Reading Priscilla Dann-Courtney's personal anecdotes and observations is like listening to soothing music or eating the best comfort food. Her lyrical writing style gently guides us through her insightful stories about everyday life, children, parents, and pets, and the full range of human emotions.

Amy Newmark - Publisher
Chicken Soup for the Soul

Priscilla Dann-Courtney's essays are as addictive as the buttered bagels she writes about. With her psychologist's mind, she nails the often conflicting emotions so intrinsically linked with family life today. But what blows her writing into the literary stratosphere is the poetry in these gleanings, a metaphoric vision that infuses many a dark situation with a sense of calm and well-being. What a magician!

Elisabeth Hyde - author
In The Heart of the Canyon

Priscilla Dann-Courtney's stories about the intricacies of everyday life—as a wife, as a mom, as a daughter—are by turn poignant and funny.

She paints a warm picture of her own life and connections, but in doing so, she allows us to see an almost universal experience. We all are transformed by the relationships we form and nurture around us, and it's a treat to reflect on those when traveling along Dann-Courtney's own path.

Erika Stutzman
Boulder Camera

Room To Grow
Stories of Life and Family

Priscilla Dann-Courtney Ph.D

Copyright © 2009 by Priscilla Dann-Courtney Ph.D

NorLightsPress.com
2721 Tulip Tree Rd.
Nashville, IN 47448

All rights reserved. No part of this book may be reproduced or transmitted in any form or by any means, electronic or mechanical, including photocopying, recording, or by any information storage and retrieval system, without written permission from the author, except for the inclusion of brief quotations in a review.

Printed in the United States of America

ISBN: 978-1-935254-21-8

Cover Photo: A Rocky Mountain Joe® Portrait
www.rockymountainjoe.com

Cover Design by NorLightsPress Graphics Department
Book Design by Nadene Carter

First printing, 2009

Acknowledgements

Saying, "thank-you," is one of the best parts for me. I am grateful to the many newspaper editors who took the time to read my submissions and say, "Yes!" (Barbara Ellis-*Denver Post*, Marcia Lythcott-*Chicago Tribune*, Judy Lowe-*Christian Science Monitor*, Rose Jacobius-*Washington Post*, Clay Evans, Erika Stutzman, Aimee Heckel–*Boulder Camera*.)

Thank-you to Maeve Conran and Sam Fuqua who let me read my stories on KGNU so I could experience the thrill of radio. I've known Amy Newmark (*Chicken Soup for the Soul*) since we learned to read in kindergarten. It has been an honor to share stories once again.

Thanks to the dear friends in my writing group, Valerie Grant, Anne Knorr, and Jessica McCree who finally got me to stop saying, "Well I wrote this little piece." You encouraged me to speak my voice loud and clear.

Thank you Alice Levine, my first editor after I decided to start the book journey. Your never-ending encouragement and patience with misspelled words and grammatical errors was wonderful.

Sammie Justesen, my book agent, is an Indiana angel who has been my guide from start to finish. I met those at Norlights Press in the last mile, which is always the toughest, so thank you for making it all happen.

My dear friends, Kerry and Joe Glynn will be my loving and encouraging neighbors no matter where we live. And Joe's photography has brought the beautiful pictures to so many of my columns. My 100 dear friends on my e:mail list who received my stories as they were published let me know I should keep writing. Your friendship is invaluable.

Thank you to my father for teaching me about taking risks and the importance of laughter and to my brother for reminding me that journalism is in our blood. Precious thanks to my mother and sister who are my writing role models answering emails at all hours and giving me forever thumbs up whenever I needed it.

And blessings to many yoga teachers who have given me the gift of balance, patience and inner peace. Carol Tierney taught me to celebrate myself. And my children, Ben, Max and Meara—you were my muse and I love you to the moon and back.

The final bow is to my dear husband, Joe, for letting me read out loud, always giving me plenty of room to grow.

Table of Contents

A Missed Period
    Becomes an Exclamation Point 1
Our Family Gas Station 5
Shackles and Lace 8
Shake, Rattle, and Soul 11
The Dumpster and the Cadillac. 13
My Mountain 16
A Mountain's Mourning. 19
A Mother's Run 21
Running with the Lions 25
Running In and Away 28
Hearts and Hurricanes. 32
Planes, Trains and . . . Jeans. 35
Aspen's Aspens 38
A Mother's Staycation 41
The Resolution of Silence 44
Down-Sizing to Live it Up 49
Our Home's Shelf Life 52
Got Neighbors? 54
A Family's Weave 57
Shoe and Substance Free 60
Marriage and Politics - A Cross-Examination 62
Jail and Bail 65
A New Place Named My Space 68
Sending a Text,
    Without Losing the Connection 71

Cheerleading Lessons	74
Fear and Cheer	77
Room for Cream?	81
Crimes of Ignorance	84
A Daughter's Toast to a Father's Bagel	87
Tasting Forgiveness	90
An Iron Mother	94
My Grandfather's Paper Trail	97
A Jury of One's Peers	100
Hospital Country	104
Lights Out	109
In Celebration of Colonoscopies	112
A Cookie Swap with Polish	114
77 Birthday Cakes	118
A Sweet Summer Fling	121
There's a Man in My Kitchen	124
Recollections of the Bike Centennial - Pedaling Across the Divide	127
Where U-Turns Are Legal	131
Emancipating Layla	133
Dog Paddling Pups	136
And the Envelope Please	138
Farewell to Two Men	141
Tears and Target	144
One Child Left Behind - To Become a Woman	147
A Burning Lesson	150
Our Dirty Laundry	153
Running is My Passport	156
The Housing Crisis	159
Radiating Friendship	162
Health-y Care	165
A Mother's Knitting	168
Driving Across the Divide	170

A Missed Period Becomes an Exclamation Point

Sometimes it can take years to be thankful for a gift when it arrives wrapped in sorrow. It all began five years ago on a Thursday in early November under a crisp, Colorado blue sky. I remember it was warm enough to run in shorts. As I ran, I wondered why my breasts hurt—late period, hot ears, hot breasts. At forty-five, I was new to menopause. My neighbor said, "Perhaps a pregnancy test would be a good idea."

In the small bathroom next to my psychotherapy office, I stared at two blue lines of a positive pregnancy test. I shook like a teenager in trouble. As I greeted the 9:30 patient, I knew I needed a session more than she. Afterwards I called my husband of nineteen years, the father of my three children. "It happened again—the baby thing. Could you come down here?" It was like a telegram without the words "Stop." That's how it began, and I'll always feel this was a ride I never asked to get on or off.

At our first doctor's appointment my husband and I sheepishly faced my obstetrician. "At your age miscarriage is very common." The ultrasound showed a flicker, the small heart. "The flicker is good, but you never know." Two weeks later, we arrived again.

The flicker flicked. It was my husband's forty-sixth birthday. "Happy birthday, Dad," she said, handing him a fuzzy black and white photo.

Telling the children came next. Getting the five of us together on a weekend wasn't an easy task. My fifteen-year-old had other priorities that didn't include a Saturday night family dinner. Our nine-year-old's mouth hung open and our twelve-year-old ran crying from the table after shouting, "Ever heard of birth control?" I was pulled in many directions that night as ambivalence, excitement, fear, and uncertainty seasoned the chicken and broccoli.

The CVS (chorionic villus sampling) test drew near—a test that would help determine if the baby was healthy. I could only remember the name by the drug store chain. I sat in a cold examining room watching the baby frolic on the ultra-sound screen. I was told a large needle would be inserted into my uterus to draw tissue from the placenta. Not to worry—the baby would be fine. The pain felt deep, felt wrong, then it was over. They showed me the baby again, still swimming softly. "You may have cramps, don't worry. Don't vacuum, fold laundry, or cook for 24 hours." They'd call us in two days to let us know if the baby was healthy.

I was making the kids pancakes when the phone rang. We had a healthy boy! At ten weeks, I flipped the pancakes, exhaled and decided I could survive pre-school once again.

And then another Thursday—this time melting snow marked the end of February. I proudly celebrated the three-month mark, feeling I'd made it to shore and could breathe a little easier. I sat in my doctor's waiting room surrounded by large stomachs. I placed my hands on my small stomach, embracing my child, finally willing to do it all again. I carried my baby and freshly baked coffeecake in to the doctor, thanking her for a healthy child.

She rubbed the clear "gook" on my stomach, positioning the cold doppler so we could hear the heart beat. Once again I lay peering at the ultrasound screen. I saw nothing but blackness and my doctor's shaking head. I cried, and she apologized. He was gone. Tearful nausea filled my emptiness as I fumbled with my drawstring pants. Somehow I moved to a black leather chair in her office, holding my knees to my chest, weeping like a lost child, late picking my daughter up from Brownies. My world was small snapshots after that. I drove home, conscious of my breathing as I would have during the labor I would never have.

We were instructed to arrive two hours before the necessary D&C procedure. I lay and waited as my husband worked on his laptop. A nurse arrived and introduced herself as my "cocktail waitress" for the evening. She was kind, and I cracked a smile as she patted my hand and called me "Dear." I kept talking, kept weeping, telling my "cocktail waitress" how sad I felt. Then the procedure was over and they all kindly complemented my strength. My husband held my hand as I sipped sweet grape juice. We drove home on a cold night and had to pull over. I threw up beside a stranger's driveway.

As tears welled from my empty womb, loving friends told us to plant a tree, which my husband painstakingly planted in our front yard. I bought a rock that read "Remember" and placed it in our garden. But my healing began only when I told my story on the page. Instead of the cries of a tiny newborn, I listened to my own creative voice. My writing burst forth like a baby's first breath. A tiny soul had delivered me this beautiful gift. I haven't stopped composing since I said goodbye.

Our children, even those we never meet, are truly our best teachers. Our miscarriage was not a "miss" but a carriage from the stage of procreation into a new stage of creation. With much gratitude, at age fifty my writing blossoms like the beautiful tree planted a few years ago.

Published in *Chicken Soup for the Soul: Count Your Blessings, November 2009*

Our Family Gas Station

Our kitchen often seems like a gas station with a well-worn table, comfortable chairs, and a full refrigerator. It's where each of our three children roll down the window and say, "Fill-er up please." The fill-ups began with tiny spoonfuls of rice cereal, a dollop delicately balanced on a tiny spoon. From there it went to chasing peas on the tray of a high chair, and then those pre-adolescent favorites, pepperoni hot-pockets.

My family forms a triangle, with our twenty-year-old son at one point, our seventeen-year-old son at another, and the third point is our thirteen-year-old daughter. Their kitchen check-ins, like the Bermuda triangle, bring complications and mystery of parenting. Years of conversations and family crisis have polished our table—deep emotion in the grain of the wood.

When my oldest son was sixteen, he sat down with tears held back in his large brown eyes. "Mom, there's something I've never told you guys."

I stopped twisting the top on the orange juice carton. "Really?" I answered, waiting for a blast of cold air on a winter morning.

"It's pretty bad," he added.

Now I was sliding on the icy front step. We went on

like this for a while, short phrases with no meaning. "How bad?" "Like what?" "When did it happen?" And then the gale blew through the kitchen. "I smoke cigarettes and I have for three years."

My husband walked in from work as my son described his first Lucky Strike at his middle school athletic field. It became a long night as we decided no one would leave the table until we figured out how he was going to quit. He hasn't smoked since.

My husband and I have answered the kitchen phone more than once and heard the deep voice of a police officer politely introducing himself. The most recent conversation focused on our seventeen-year-old, who'd dived from a cliff into a reservoir and then gave a false name to the green-clad forest ranger who questioned him. Once again the kitchen table became a "pit stop" we all would have preferred to drive by. It was a chase for honesty instead of peas on a tray. We also service softer needs like when my daughter arrives home, asking for eyeliner, a new school binder and seven friends to sleepover immediately.

The list of needs and wants in our gas station is varied, making us wish we had a third parent "attendant" to give us support and guidance when the emotional mechanics become complicated. How old does one have to be to get hair highlights? How long does a parent wait to check in again with a college son, after one phone call where he tearfully says his course load is killing him? How involved do you get when your daughter mentions a girl in her math class who has cuts all over her arm?

And then there are times when business is slow. The quiet leaves my husband and me alone to attend to ourselves; to fill up on the connections we lost while caring for children. Someday they will have to fill up on their own. There will be no attendant at the window. But I hope they know our kitchen will never shut down. The fuel of love never runs out.

Published in the
Christian Science Monitor, August 2007

Shackles and Lace

Last Friday morning was snowing and freezing—the morning I spent in juvenile court. I didn't know what to wear. This was the same feeling I had when I met with a bondsman to bail our cleaning lady out of jail. I had work clothes and play clothes, but legal clothes seemed different. I chose a blouse with lace around the collar—a border of innocence framing my mother guilt. I am guilty of raising a 16 year-old son who dove from a cliff into a reservoir. When approached by a green clad forest ranger, he lied about his name. Suddenly he became Ryan Oliver, which is a felony—impersonating with intent to harm another. He knows no one named Ryan Oliver, but last June the law didn't care about that, as my son stood dripping in his wet swimsuit.

We drove tentatively toward the courthouse on icy streets, anxious about arriving late and anxious about arriving at all. We didn't fight until we pulled into the parking lot and suddenly I became "irritating." By the time we reached courthouse security, we both passed through the metal detector in silence. I wondered if it would detect the metallic hardness of my anger. We headed toward courtroom P; brushing elbows, we forgave each other. We met our lawyer in the hall, since we'd learned felonies require an attorney. Our children had gone to pre-school together, where there was a "goodbye window" so we could send kisses to our kids. My son's pre—school tears had been large enough to wash the windowsill. As we discussed with our lawyer, hope for the diversion program, I remembered the sparkle in my son's eyes when he finally learned to dive. Often in trying to be encouraging, I've said, "just dive in!" Except—sometimes not.

When we opened the doors to juvenile court, the room was smaller than I expected. Perhaps like desks in elementary school, the room grows according to age. We found our seats among other families, all guilty of various crimes, many of us speaking different languages. But we were all similar in our willingness to show up for our children, wishing we didn't have to. The silence came back between my son and me. We were both treading water, buoyed by feelings we didn't want to share. Especially my son, who needed me now, when he preferred to believe parents weren't all that important. Some of the accused appeared in orange jumpsuits and shackles, some wore a shirt and tie. My son, along with others, kept their ski jackets on as if to say, "just stopping in, won't be here long."

We sat uncomfortably listening to the judge call out names one by one. He'd say a name and the accused person and parent would sheepishly approach the podium. He'd take a minute to read his notes, sigh, and then glare at the fidgeting offender. "Now, Miss Lawrence you seem to have ignored your boyfriend's restraining order, and please remove your gum." "Mr. Gardner, do you know it's a felony to destroy government property with graffiti. Now wouldn't that disrupt your football career?" We never made it to the podium, since we were in the group the prosecutor recommended for diversion. Like sheep excused from being sheered, we were herded into another room to be educated about the diversion program—which allows restitution through community service. After six months, the offense is expunged from the record. So my son will continue his volunteer work teaching arts and crafts to developmentally disabled adults and pay back the lawyers fees over time.

We stopped for bagels at the courthouse café, tasting a more peaceful silence. I dropped him at school, where he smiled and said, "Mom, thanks for the lift."

Parenting is a series of "goodbye windows" where no matter how bad the driving, we always return to pick up our children. My own tears washed the steering wheel as I turned back into the flow of traffic.

Published in the
Denver Post, May 2008

Shake, Rattle, and Soul

Since I'll be turning 50 soon, I thought it was time to take a yoga class—hoping to spend my next 50 years a little calmer. So one morning I stopped into a new yoga center in town, where a gentle woman offered me a cup of tea. I sipped slowly—a tiny taste of peace, which encouraged me to return for the evening class. Six months later, everyone in my family has become accustomed to "Mom's" yoga. They patiently watch me in strange poses on the living room floor, my son stepping over me to reach for his sneakers, my daughter whispering, "When you're done, what's for dinner?"

But they were apprehensive when I considered spending four days at a yoga retreat. "Mom, you're not going to begin chanting are you?" asked my son. I was concerned about important things like, would they have coffee?

When I called to make my reservation, the woman who answered the phone had a voice as calming as my yoga teacher's. My hope was to sound like that someday. So one morning in May, I flew to a mountain setting in Sedona in search of my own peaceful voice. Each day we learned new poses, breathing, and healing techniques. I soon learned our teachers were not saying, "Retard" as we changed positions, but

"Return." I found "retard" comforting; it had just meant go slow, which I did. Soon we began looking into one another's eyes instead of at our nametags. Our teachers told us, "It is our eyes that tell our true story." We learned to chew our food 30 times. I learned to take bigger bites of banana to make it last longer. Our yoga practice helped us experience a universal energy our teachers carried like a tray of delicious fruits.

On the last night, when I awoke to the ground shaking, I decided to eat a rice cake. I fell back asleep, and a few hours later awoke to the same trembling earth. And then I knew. The vibration, the energy, was within me. I sat up and did what the teachers told me. Focus and breathe. That was wiser than eating a rice cake.

When I first arrived I was homesick for my Colorado home. By the end, I found home trembling in my bed, but scared of nothing. I had found my soul-er power within and my own peaceful voice.

To my son's relief, his mom didn't return home chanting. But I did return home changed. Yoga camp is a scavenger hunt for one's soul. Our sweat and tears hold the clues of hope. I now drink brown rice tea and not coffee. Each day I find time to lie with my feet in the air and breath. I place my yoga classes into my schedule like soft cushions fluffing up my life. It used to be that when I removed my headphones from my small pink i-pod, the music would stop. But now my soul's quiet melody continues. And to think it all began with a warm cup of tea one January morning.

Published in
Body & Brain Magazine, September 2006

The Dumpster and the Cadillac

*I*t was a cold Friday night, so I had to wear socks to bed. Our family is at the developmental stage where my husband and I go to sleep before our three children. Never a deep sleep until they're home for good, but nevertheless we are under the covers before them. Ten p.m. and the phone rang—closer to my husband's head, he answered, "Hello...oh are you okay?" I was definitely awake, alert, worried within seconds. My sixteen-year-old son had proudly possessed his license for a day.

"Is it drivable?" my groggy husband asked.

Simultaneously my stomach sank, my chest got tight and I let out a "mother" sigh passed down from my own mother that she'd inherited from her mother. The story was, our son was soberly returning from a party, too nervous to drive on main roads, reporting he thought he'd get stopped for being too young to drive. Like the heavy woman who loses weight and still sees an overweight body, adolescents may be old enough for a license but inside they may feel they're in elementary school. Driving around a corner, he met his first patch of ice that glided him quickly and smoothly into a large, black dumpster. The dumpster sustained no injury, but my son's pride was totaled. "You have to punish me big time!" he announced upon arriving home.

It seemed easier to start dealing with the insurance company immediately instead of on Monday morning when I'd be put on hold, listening to slow jazz. I dialed the number as my son searched through a messy kitchen drawer for the gray duct tape that would be color coordinated with the bashed silver fender. Since we'd be driving the car for at least two more days, it helped if we didn't have heavy metal pieces jutting out over the front tire. Just as seeing a band-aid instead of an open wound draws less attention, layers of tape might be less conspicuous

When Monday morning arrived, I had the job of car delivery to the auto-body shop. The Enterprise rental car was coordinated so I'd be picked up at the Honda service center. There was something game like about the plans. Without the small notes of a scavenger hunt, I was directed from one location to the next.

As I stood shivering in the parking lot waiting for my rental car to arrive, a large silver Cadillac pulled in. The driver, in tie and pressed shirt with an Enterprise logo, smiled widely. I didn't smile quite as widely, but I opened the passenger side door and squashed down into a soft, gray seat.

"Nice car, don't you think Ms. Courtney?" my driver beamed.

"Very." I didn't know what else to say except I hoped the drive was quick and I saw no one I knew.

"For just a few dollars more, I'll give you an upgrade."

"Oh, no, that's okay." I was polite and prayed we'd have no more discussion about the gas-guzzling car. We'd recently purchased a Prius, which is like driving around with a bumper sticker that says, "Aren't you proud of us? We're democrats."

The paper work was quick. With a smile, my driver handed me the keys, then winked and added, "This is your lucky day. I upgraded you, no charge." Now we had a problem. I felt much more comfortable in the duct taped Honda. A week in a Cadillac was a death sentence. My thoughts jumped from fears about people confusing my politics, to my husband not allowing it in the garage. Would it even fit in the garage? And how would I duck down low and also see over the steering wheel? I drove slowly out of the parking lot, breathing deeply. My yoga teacher's voice in my head calmed my fears.

I made it to work without sideswiping anyone. I maneuvered into my parking space, opened the door, stepped down to the pavement and quickly walked away from the vehicle. It beeped when I pressed the lock button on the unfamiliar key chain.

My day at the office was challenging, but not as challenging as facing the car again in the darkened parking lot.!"

As I pulled into the driveway, I hoped the neighbors would just think relatives were visiting. I'd warned my family earlier in the day about my impending arrival. My husband's response was, "Oh, God." In just a few days the discussion in our kitchen had gone from dumpster to Cadillac. I try and teach my children that labels on clothing and brand names aren't who we are. So for the next week I learned my soul needed to shine through, even behind the wheel of a Cadillac. I hope my son learned the importance of driving slowly and safely. But I think his mother learned something more. As long as one remains straight and proud in the driver's seat of our lives—our Cadillacs and hybrids become incidental.

My Mountain

I ski alone; not because I have to, but because I want to. My mother says, "Oh, dearie, you're not all alone on the slopes, are you?" She's 80 and I'm almost 50, yet she still worries about me as if I'm a teenager behind the wheel. I never tell her I prefer to be alone so I can hear the "whoosh" of my skis. When I stop, the quiet wraps around me to make me even warmer.

I began skiing on pink plastic skis at the age of five, on a chair lift in Vermont where our skis touched the ground the whole ride up. I was tiny enough for my mother to straddle me between her legs, my skis lined up against hers, safe and happy. With time, my red rubber boots became black leather tie boots safety strapped to small wooden skis. Lessons and more lessons on family ski vacations might have primed others for Turin, but instead I was trained to just enjoy the experience.

So decades later I appreciate the slopes and solitude every Friday morning. For those hours I am no longer a mother of three, a clinical psychologist lending a trained ear, or even a loving wife. For that moment I am just me, challenged by moguls instead of questions of parenting; greeted by lift attendants instead of a client's tears, and embraced by a small mountain instead of my husband. Sometimes I allow another rider to share my chair. Their personalities range from a Nederland police chief, to a pair of teenagers planning their next "bowl," a computer executive who lost me after firewall and modem, and a gym teacher from North Dakota. We make conversation, talking into our bundled scarves, hands stuffed into mittens tucked between knees. We wish each other a good day and with relief I am alone again.

Often the wind is cold, the sun somewhere else, but my focus on staying warm keeps me looking inside. The view outside is secondary. Yet when I drive up the canyon, round the last bend into Nederland, the view of white, weaving slopes calms me. From a distance, the snow always looks good and the wind is absent. I drive slowly, never wanting a police by my window to disrupt my peace. I pass the coffee shop nestled in a train car and look forward to my coffee on the way home, with plenty of room for cream.

Sometimes I think this time I'll take an hour lesson, to really learn the bumps. But then I'd be in relationship with someone, even if it was only an hour, and we'd have to talk. I don't think I could share a chair for that long. Friends say I should do "Women's Wednesday." I'm overwhelmed by the thought, flashing back to a crowded hallway in middle school.

So I continue to drive up the canyon alone. Sometimes I treat myself to no music, letting silence spin its own melody. I ski as fast as the morning passes. And then I am back in my front seat, scrunched and awkwardly pulling off my ski gear. I run a brush through my hair, but I don't care how I look. I turn my car down the mountain with the same rhythm I had on the slopes. I slide into a parking space; the bell jingles as I open the coffee shop door, and I am home. Slices of orange sweeten the taste of creamy coffee. I try and figure out all the ingredients of their blueberry muffin so I can make some at home. And then I read the Friday section of the newspaper, relishing that the weekend has just begun. And then I write, creating stories and conversation on the page. A small circle of woman are often there, knitting together. We trade smiles; their colorful yarn ties me gently to their small group. I smile goodbye to the blond lady behind the counter, holding my books and feeling like a schoolgirl. I'm grown up by the time I drive into Boulder, and I'm ready for my life again.

Everyone should have a mountain, they can call their own.

Published in the
Boulder Camera, December 2006

A Mountain's Mourning

*L*ast Tuesday's wind blew our morning paper—and my mind. After a sleepless night, a chaotic run with our bounding golden retriever, and discovering our recyclables in the neighbor's yard, the morning felt a little unruly. But while many of us were dealing with windy inconvenience, Eldora Mountain was shattered by terror and trauma. A disturbed employee shot and killed an adored general manager. Suddenly the inconvenience of a windy morning was a welcome breeze compared to such a tornado of grief.

Eldora Mountain holds the wonder of my family's growing up. Weekend mornings I'd drag my children to ski lessons, often still in pajamas as they groaned about how "stupid" lessons were. Thankfully they'd be goggled and snowsuited by the time we arrived. Sometimes they loved it; sometimes they didn't—often leaving me haggard and fearful we'd be the one Colorado family who didn't ski. Years later they've all found their way, either by skis or snowboard, and I'm left with the beauty of skiing alone.

When I chose to ski the day after the tragedy, I arrived to a somber wake on skis under a clear blue sky. The lift attendants and the employees were the family left behind, all victims in their own way. No yellow tape identified the crime scene, but unseen tapes in the minds of shattered victims who saw red against pure white snow will be a never forgotten marker. In medical emergencies, people sometimes call out, "Is there a doctor in the house?" But in the aftermath of a trauma, we need compassionate listeners to hear the voices of the frightened and grieving. I will contribute to the fund listed in the paper, but I also felt the need to contribute some kindness toward a mountain, in memory of a man I'd never met and his young family left behind. Pushing the soft scarf away from my face, I shared my condolences with the young woman checking my pass.

"Thanks. I was there and I haven't slept."

The hatless lift operator answered, "It's just overwhelming and I can't find my footing."

A pale woman shoveling snow nodded and hung her head.

It would be easy to say the psychologist in me wanted to lend an ear. But in truth, that wasn't it. Eldora has always been a healing, meditative place for me—a woman, a wife, a mother who cherishes solitude on a snowy mountain. It was gratitude that encouraged me to reach out to strangers, hoping my small gesture might make for a warmer "mourning"- as we all try to grapple with the contrast of a black death against the white purity of a ski slope where we all go to play.

None of us ski alone, and when a storm of this magnitude blows in, we have to heed the advice of the slanting sign at Eldora, "Please Double Up Due to Windy Conditions." And sometimes we have to ride triple before we can learn to play again.

Published in the
Denver Post, January 2009

A Mother's Run

My mother once asked, "What would happen if everyone just stopped running?" Not in the metaphorical sense, but in the "Nike" way, just no more joggers. I on the other hand started at sixteen and have never stopped.

My routine every morning is to make the beds half dressed, and then I don worn purple shorts and sweatshirt, and close the front door behind me. I never say goodbye; everyone knows where I'm going. I begin slowly, hopping over newspapers not taken in yet. I tuck my fists into my sleeves, cozy in a sweatshirt that has lived with me for more than fifteen years. I have a variety of routes, never deciding which direction until my feet hit the pavement. I have passed the same runners for years; the elderly man with two black poodles who now runs alone because his poodles have grown too old; the balding man whose dog can never keep up; the Latino woman with a phone headset chatting away in Spanish; the woman who runs on her toes in red spandex tights; the older woman who always walks with her coffee mug; and the lanky man who's often doing sprints up one of the hills. We pass smiles between us, like relay batons.

Much of the year I just run, not worrying about

speed. However as March fades and April lands, I try and pick up the pace. Summer racing begins with the Bolder Boulder, a 10K race boosting 45,000 runners. Years ago the waves were single letters, never completing the alphabet. Now we have the "B", "BB", "BA", "QQ", and "ZZZ". Consonants and vowels pinned to our shirts, we smile with the prestige of those early alphabetical letters, the "qualifying waves."

Although early April allows me two months to gain speed, I always worry this might be the year I wear my older age of 46 instead of a proud "A" or "B." This year feels different. I finally have a child running. Not that we'll run side-by-side, sweating encouraging words. Only when a child can keep my pace or surpass me would I allow a mother-child team. No one seems to expect me do the "good" mother thing and just slow down. My son will run with a friend and the friend's "good" mother. Of course I worry he'll get lost amid the throngs of runners and cheering fans. He's the one out of the three who always roamed, only to be lost on a ski slope or in a mall. He now has a tiny cell phone for these occasions. I'd love for him to just slide it into his shorts. Unfortunately this mother worry still isn't strong enough for me to slow up and run together.

The event provides a truly old time community atmosphere where roads are blocked off, with folding chairs on sidewalks, bands, belly dancers, waving flags, and Air Force jets against blue skies. For a brief moment we all feel we're in an imagined time long ago. The weather always seems to register as a participant. There have been years of rain where green trash bags protect you at the start, only to be discarded at the 1/4 mile mark. At times the heat is so oppressive, you pray for a breeze like you do the next mile marker. And sometimes we have those glorious in-between days when you awaken at 6:00 a.m. to a blue, crisp morning.

There is such relief when the day arrives. Transportation has been organized. The coverage of younger siblings is done. Plans of where to watch for cheering friends has been finalized. A special part of race morning is—I actually get to shower before I sweat.

The start line is full of runners stretching out their anticipation with squats and toe touches. This is almost like stage fright, wanting to run away before the curtain rises. The relief is, we all get to do just that—run away with abandon.

I think of my son a few waves behind. Like me, he calculated when he wants to cross the finish line, and like me, if he doesn't, brief disappointment will follow. Like me, he will run a proud time. They no longer begin the race with a startling gunshot. Out of respect for peace and nonviolence, a waving flag allows troops of runners to find peace within during the next six miles.

As always, my first mile is too fast, but my rhythm develops with corner drums and guitars as back up. The finish is in the CU stadium, where each of us can pretend for a moment we have the heart of an Olympian. My time makes me happy; my son's finishing face makes me happier.

The trek home is always a little challenging, given the race finishes a good four miles from the start. Numbered runners and their snack bags wait for buses that may never come. I'm lucky enough to have a husband who comes to find me. After dropping him back home, I return to help stranded runners. Strangers I've never met trustingly hop into my vehicle and accept a ride home. On any other day I might not be trusted, and I might be skeptical of a sweaty stranger waiting for a bus. This small gesture of mine wraps up my morning like a ribbon on a gift.

The next morning I slip back into my running shoes and the comfort of just another morning run. There is always a childlike excitement to read the Citizens' Results in the newspaper. As I've grown older, I squint a little more to read the tiny printed names of the first 2000 men and women across the finish line. My heart races as I carefully count my place among other 46-year-old women. This year I shout from the kitchen table, waking any family members enjoying those last pillow minutes. Hands in the air, I squeak out, "I was first!" My husband beams as I check just to make sure the tiny print isn't tricking me. This morning run will feel like my own victory lap. This will not be the day they all stop running. I know my mother would never want that. Some day she'll run this race. Perhaps when she's 80, so she too can celebrate the Olympian within.

Published in
the *Boulder Camera*, May 2003

Running with the Lions

I've run every morning for years. Like brushing my teeth, it is just part of my morning routine. My only companion is my golden retriever, and sometimes I don't even let her join me. On those mornings she is rescued by my husband, who allows her to walk with him. The only problem arises if the two of them meet me on the trail; then poor Layla stands between us like a child with divorced parents. How can she choose? But the comfort and security of my morning has been disrupted lately. Warnings about both mountain lions and rattlesnakes are posted at our familiar trailheads.

One morning Layla and I were enjoying the early morning coolness when she found a friend to play with—a silvery fat, coiled snake. Like many dangerous situations, they happen quickly. One minute you're musing about having to stop at the cleaners, and then you're hysterically screaming—fearing death. Layla gleefully jumped at the snake's tongue, believing it was a skinny version of her stuffed dog toy that hissed instead of squeaked. All our hard work at puppy class was left behind with the teacher and his clicker. I don't think shrieking out your dog's name in-between tears was one of the commands. Layla continued this run close—run away game, oblivious of any danger. But I believe the snake responded to the high decimal of my voice, which served as a momentary distraction, just long enough for me to grab Layla's collar and drag her to safety. We're still working on "voice control" in off-leash areas. Shamefully the only being that seemed to manage any self-control in that situation was the snake.

That was the snake morning and now I wonder if we will have a lion morning. The newspaper did print clear rules of etiquette when meeting a mountain lion for the first time. I have them memorized, but if I can follow them when experiencing high stress is another concern. I hope my snake performance isn't an indication of my behavior if I meet a lion. The primary rule is "Don't Run." I hope my freeze response will kick in, because it probably goes along with my panic response. Then, "No eye contact." That seems easy enough. Although I do try to honestly connect with people, eye to eye, I assume I won't be trying to build a meaningful connection with the lion. Then, "Be as big as you can." For example, hold you're backpack over your head. I can't recall ever taking a backpack on a morning run and anyone who knows me will agree, "big" isn't how I would describe myself. Maybe on the inside, but no lion really cares about my emotional strength and soul's journey. And then, "If attacked, fight back." I would do that, because I worry about the trauma for my children if they had to cope with their mother being eaten by a lion. None of these rules make me feel any safer running my trails on a blue-sky morning.

As I climb higher, my heart rate increases, maybe because of fear more than the slow incline. I find myself checking back over my shoulder and trying to be alert to movement in the distance. I'm comforted by seeing other runners and often ask, "Seen any mountain lions?" One man explained the increase in lion sightings is all about balancing out the ecosystem—more deer, more lions. Another runner taught me the difference between a bull snake and a rattler. So I am certainly more educated about my wildlife neighbors. I'm willing to share my open space, and perhaps I could communicate that to these creatures if they let me look into their eyes. But I know the rules, so I'll continue my morning ritual with a little sweat and a lot of prayer that our lions also value world peace.

Running In and Away

*I*t is a cool September morning—swapping seasons as I don my worn Nike sweatshirt for warmth, on my early morning run. So begins a long weekend away for my husband and me, as we head up to the Shambhalya Mountain Center (600 acres in Red Feather Lakes) two hours outside of Boulder, Colorado, for a three-day retreat, "Running with the Mind of Meditation." I encouraged us to sign up after meeting Mark Plaatjes, former Olympic runner and physical therapist. I lay on his physical therapy table, trying to explain my knee was feeling "not right." Thankfully he assured me it was nothing serious, as he attacked and stretched my knees and quads. He explained that as we age, collagen in our muscles loses elasticity and builds up, making us more prone to injury. Thus at 50, I was suffering from congealed collagen. As our conversation continued in-between painful, yet healing breaths, he discussed the merits of yoga. He explained yoga is extremely helpful for runners because it keeps our collagen more elastic and increases both range of motion and blood flow. "Runners notoriously don't stretch enough!" Yoga can help with that. So when I read about a fall workshop combining running, yoga and meditation—my husband and I signed on.

I tell my neighbor we're leaving for a weekend of running and meditation. She smiles and says, "Isn't that an oxymoron?" For runners, it's a beautiful metaphor.

As we drive out of town, the aspens are just beginning to turn golden. The Shambhalya Center doesn't allow cell phones, Internet access or dogs. The first two are a welcome simplicity. But I think about my running companion, Layla, who would love to frolic in such freedom. However, she and our three children have been left behind to wonder, yet again, why their parents hold such strange poses and have kept running shoes by the door ever since they can remember.

We meet our running/meditation colleagues, who've come from as far as Holland, Seattle, Canada and Arkansas. We enjoy a tasty meal of tofu and vegetables, with plenty of hot tea. We share training and race stories and we contemplate the weekend ahead of us. It feels like a running/meditation sleep-away camp with enlightened counselors.

The first morning a small group of us, breathing into cold hands, plan a short trail run. We are then welcomed by an hour of yoga, stretching in ways that remind us we should do this more often. A gentle yoga teacher trained in the Anusara tradition works with us, in a class specifically designed for the everyday runner. Then we sit, breathe and meditate, preparing for an afternoon with Sakyong Mipham Rinpoche, a renowned Tibetan spiritual leader and marathoner, who will instruct us on how to bring the East and West together on mountain trails. Finding the peaceful warrior within enhances the powerful warrior wearing running shoes.

He discusses the NYC marathon, when a reporter asked him if he had time to meditate before the race. He answered, "Oh, no. I will meditate during!"

As he instructs us in sitting meditation where we must focus and be mindful of the breath, he points out that running meditation is a broader mindfulness. Our focus is on our step—repetitive "heal" to toe, repetitive breath—in and out, upright posture—aligning our spines. Tranquility of the mind comes from this body mindfulness, returning the gift of strength and endurance to our running practice. It reminds me of running with my golden retriever who can go off trail, like my mind travels away. I must call her back, as I must harness my thoughts within.

The next morning is a group run with Rinpoche, who stands among us in a T-shirt and shorts—his ceremonial Tibetan gown left in the closet. This is a spiritual 10K, not a race, but an attempt to e-rase life's distracting thoughts, such as, *did my daughter make it to her 8th grade cheerleading practice* and *is my 17- year-old son being responsible*?

The morning is blue sky gorgeous. The run begins at 8400 feet on a mountain trail whose beauty makes a runner's mouth water. We're encouraged to run in silence, listening for an inner quiet, a peaceful solitude we all share. Like life, there are ups and downs and we must not look too far ahead—we will lose our footing in the present. When we hit an uphill—we just keep going. We may encounter horse manure along the way, and sometimes we have to get our feet wet in mountain streams. We're encouraged not to compare ourselves to others. This is an individual journey and we all end up in the same place anyway—which in this case was the Great Stupa, a Tibetan sacred monument dedicated to universal peace and compassion.

Gatorade and bananas decorate our entry into the sacred shrine recently blessed by the Dalai Lama.

We breathe in the tranquility as we stretch our sore quads. Moments of enlightenment do not substitute for the reality of creaky knees after miles logged over the past 35 years. Our victory lap is a slow walk around the Stupa. The day ends with words of wisdom on how to train our mind and body to "run" our lives with greater peace and compassion

As we drive home the following morning, a few more aspens have turned—the golden transition of seasons carrying us back into our lives. I will always remember the words of Ripoche, who with a glint in his eye, said, "And then they brought me a treadmill while at the monastery." That image will always remind me that if a treadmill can be brought to a monastery, we can certainly bring a monastery's sacred tranquility to the treadmill of our lives.

Published in
FitYoga, August 2008

Hearts and Hurricanes

My husband and I are rookies when it comes to travel. We shyly stay in the United States and only recently ventured to Mexico. In contrast, I grew up in a family where travel was one of the four food groups—good health demanded it. We spent summers voyaging to Paris on the Queen Mary, picnicking in the English countryside, and watching tremendous men throw logs the size of Redwood trees at the Scottish Highland games. At six years old, I found nothing about this interesting, romantic or beautiful. I spent a lot of time just wanting a hot dog. The youngest of three children, I was squashed in the back seat between my brother and sister, feeling carsick and dreading the next castle. Inevitably I felt lost in large groups of foreigners, listening to a French guide point to doorways and furniture in excited tones. Castles smelled like a mixture of my father's starchy shirts and musty closets. In between museums, my mother read to us from green Michelin guidebooks as my father drove haltingly forward on a different side of the road. Like the guides, she too would get excited, interjecting, "Isn't that fascinating?' like a chorus, hoping we'd sing along.

Decades later, I'm trying to find my own sweet melody in travel as my husband and I venture away each year without children—in search of moments lost during the rewarding, yet excruciating labor of parenting. Our recent trip to California wine country began with yellow sticky notes on the kitchen counter for my friend who'd be minding the kids. The notes held reminders of times for two tennis lessons, one dentist appointment, my son's volunteer work with developmentally disabled adults, two Halloween parties, one school field trip, garbage pick-up and plant watering. Puppy care, bunny care and fish feeding had their own full page.

We were almost ready to leave on our trip when the unexpected happened: A Florida hurricane hit my son's university and my father in-law had triple bypass surgery.

Suddenly my organized sticky notes held no comfort, no direction. When I was making reservations at our Mendocino Bed and Breakfast, I hadn't taken into account older hearts and young hurricanes. Like the lines in the airline magazines, showing all routes, all possible destinations, I felt pulled apart. My son was driving north, my father in-law was ailing in the south, and we were considering going west.

My father advised, "Go west, your son will be fine."

My mother said, "Stay home, you should be there."

My husband was pondering traveling to a southern ICU, leaving me with a lot of crossed out sticky notes. If I listened to my heart, I needed to get away. As I zipped my suitcase, guilt was stuffed into the corners next to a good novel and my running shoes. We were going anyway, with charged cell phones, Internet access and the hope our self-care wouldn't impinge on hurricane winds and recovering hearts.

We landed on a cool, rainy San Francisco runway. The Hertz lady had black eyelashes as long as her sleek nails. I was more concerned about the color of the car and delighted to be standing beside my husband with no one asking me for anything. We wove north on Route 1, finding a radio station that played the old songs from when we were in ninth grade.

After stopping in Santa Rosa for tofu and vegetables, a shared glass of wine, a cup of de-caf coffee, and a shared chocolate chip cookie, we were feeling the safety of an adolescent relationship where you and me get a little fuzzy. Without children, we were free to be children. The Mendocino coast facilitates the coming together of redwoods, rocky cliffs and a quiet blue ocean. The stillness of the forest on morning runs matched the inner stillness of our solitude. In our regular life, my husband and I have gotten used to running separately. Young children demanded "revolving door" jogging. He'd return through the front door and I'd head out the back. He usually did the early run because he felt more comfortable with a headlamp—but no revolving doors in Mendocino.

Daily calls to the civilization of responsibilities kept us informed about heart and hurricane realities. Power to the university campus was restored, my father in-law's pacemaker working well.

There are no sticky notes on vacation and stepping out of a morning shower has no deadline. We hit more coffee shops and bakeries than wineries. Heading home, our suitcase zipped more easily because we had no guilt stuffed in the corners. Everyone survived. And I am reminded of the importance of making our pace slower—it strengthens the heart in a marriage. So tomorrow, when the winds blow again, we're that much stronger to take care and hold tight. And someday, we might even make it to a French castle.

Planes, Trains and . . . Jeans

I turned 52 in Atlanta, Georgia. It wasn't in the plan, but two feet of spring snow in Denver grounded us in Georgia while returning from Florida. The smiley man at Starbucks gave me a free piece of crumb cake and tea.

"My, you're just a youngin'!" his southern drawl warming my morning.

I'd never been to Georgia before, so I pulled out my laptop just to view a U.S. map. Plum on top of Florida—I realized we hadn't gotten far. My daughter wasn't interested in a geography lesson, a day in Atlanta, or anything less than a direct flight home! And my husband had no luck finding a healthy looking apple from an airport vendor. We weren't exactly rolling with the punches.

The MARTA quickly became the excitement as we learned Atlanta has an excellent inner city transit system. We had the choice of the aquarium, the Coca-Cola Museum, CNN, or a four-story mall. One look at my daughter made it clear. The only substitute for a direct flight home was a direct route to a mall. Rainy and gray outside—I was comforted by the weather as our train bumped a long. In contrast, Boulder has only a sprinkle of rainy days. I could also cherish being in the minority. While Boulder's landscape may be varied and colorful, our population is not.

The quest became a new pair of jeans for my daughter. We were choosing indulgence at this point, trying to sooth our disappointment over what actually was a minor inconvenience—we weren't exactly stranded without food and water. Jeans that cost as much as a round-trip plane ticket were piled high against the wall in the back of the store. My gasp alerted the young woman behind the counter.

"You see ,they're made in California, they're very durable and if a zipper breaks we'll just give you a new pair," she justified.

Her small hips were wrapped in perfectly fitting jeans that she must have gotten at cost—a less expensive plane ticket. A wide smiling woman with wider hips nudged me and in quiet tones encouraged,

"Filene's Basement hon', just across the street. Only way to go."

I nudged my daughter and we were on our way to Filene's. Having no roots and nowhere to be allowed us to live simply, focusing only on a good deal for a pair of jeans. This turned into a birthday scavenger hunt like those we invented for the kids when they were young. Racks of jeans welcomed us instead of the perfectly piled jean wall. My husband patiently found a chair and the "trying on" began. Jean shopping is a specific type of shopping. Fit is the focus, and only the woman in the mirror knows for sure. After a quick ten minutes ,my daughter appeared out of the dressing room with a definitive nod. The dollop of icing came with a 20% discount.

Bumping back to the airport by train, I smiled about my birthday celebration. What a way to bring in my new year. Fly somewhere new for a day, go on a scavenger hunt, celebrate with a piece of crumble cake, take a train ride, a plane ride, and wrap it all up with the magic of spontaneity. May I live the next fifty years with less planning and more appreciation for surprise landings.

Aspen's Aspens

The aspens in autumn are golden comfort for our eyes—so wonderful; just one color is all we need. One early morning as I run up Aspen Mountain, the ground is damp after a cool rain, yellow leaves leaving fossil-like imprints in my path. At my turn around point I'm welcomed by a view that has been quietly behind me, pushing me higher.

This is an October weekend getaway my husband and I cherish to ease our busy lives.

We leave straight from the office on Thursday evening, driving I-70 in darkness and headlights. We make it to Vail in an hour and forty minutes, driving the speed limit. No traffic or children quicken the drive. Leaving behind two children and a puppy over Homecoming weekend took weeks of planning for responsible coverage.

My daughter was sure to remind me, "You guys are ridiculous. No other parents do this sort of thing!"

I appease my guilt with, "Perhaps it's why we are still married."

Aspen is quiet in October, breathing easier after the summer, and about to inhale for winter. After a summer of too many plane trips visiting family, we wanted to go somewhere without security checkpoints and where we could carry our own toothpaste. There is no official time change, but time does change. We suddenly hold time in our own hands. We let go of being wrapped by the hands of our daily time clock. Friday morning, I'm running at 8:30 a.m. instead of backing out of the driveway. We splurge on massages, hoping to find the masseuse who walked on my back during a summer conference in June. I overhear a conversation about the rose colored walls at the spa. "They calm people who come in angry." Perhaps the world needs more rose-colored walls. We meander through the day with no to-do lists.

Saturday, I awake early to do yoga in front of a picture window framed by the rustling aspens—leaves I've adopted as my weekend mascot. If I got organized quickly enough I could jog to Aspen High School for a 5K I read about. I don't want to and I do want to—a racer's ambivalence stretching through me as I reach for my toes. At almost 50, I'm trying to remove the "push" from within that contains the unwelcome sidebar of pressure. I stay in my pose long enough to feel the luxury of no start line, at least for this Saturday morning. Aspen Mountain welcomes me again and I run up until my body has had enough—a lovely push without pressure.

We eat breakfast bagels at noon and wander through the Aspen Saturday market, passing up the squash and tomatoes, cherishing the fact that we won't be cooking. We magically find Colorado peaches in October, "a new breed" the smiling vendor assures us, rubbing her cold hands together. The roasting green chilies look delicious; the smell tricking us into believing it's fine to smoke pot anywhere in Aspen. The weather changes quickly—cool, rainy, sunny, and back again. Blue sky is over rated. Before lunch I get a pedicure at a small shop as my husband reads Newsweek. We find time to see movies and watch TV, luxuries that escape us during the week.

The NY Times is at our door Sunday morning, and we are in heaven. As we drive out of town, I stop at a French bakery with the best banana bread I'd ever tasted. I ask the mustached man behind the counter if he might share the recipe. He quietly confers with the baker behind him, French accents wafting over the counter. He turns back to me, "So sorry, but he has his secrets."

As we head home over Independence Pass, light rain turning to snow, I wonder about the secret ingredient in Aspen we've visited over and over for the last 25 years. I decide it must be somewhere hidden in the leaves.

Published in
the *Boulder Camera*, September 2007

A Mother's Staycation

Summers have always been a time for family vacations, along with one week away where I travel single, finding a professional conference that gives me the gift of solitude. But like many families, finances made this summer different. Instead, I search for vacation moments in day to day living, seeking hidden leisure without the luxury of travel. I challenge myself to leave daily rituals and routines behind without packing a suitcase. Just for a moment I try not sweeping the kitchen floor, wiping a sticky counter or reading the newspaper—things I escape while on vacation. Instead, I run a race or attend a friend's book reading, a concert, a yoga class, cherish buying peaches at the farmers market and read the NYTimes at a coffee-shop each morning during my week. Putting together a week's stolen moments of leisure equals a nurturing vacation.

As we stay at home this summer, family and visitors spend their holiday eating quiche and salad at our table, their suitcases overflowing in our guest room. Their comings and goings give me the illusion of movement. As a passenger on a plane that's backing out of a gate, buildings seem to move before we realize we're the ones in transit. For this summer, we remain standing while others move in and out of our family circle.

On a recent warm Saturday morning, I cherished the cool air on my bus ride after yoga class. Not having the car relieved me of chauffer duty, making it easier to shed the floppy summer hat of motherhood and pretend just for the morning that I was on vacation. My farmer's market peaches sat next to me, like a sweet friend along for the ride. As my Saturday turned in to Sunday, I drove toward Allens Park before the kids were out of bed—their evenings now languish late into the night way after my husband and I have settled in. The beauty of Longs Peak towering against a strikingly blue sky reminds me I too can be a vacationer as I follow the Virginia license plate ahead of me. My ears pop, announcing I'm climbing higher and warn me that this 10K race at 8600 ft. may not be one of my better times.

I left my watch on the bathroom sink. As a psychologist my day is blocked out in to 45-minute intervals. Today, I cherish freedom without the hands of time wrapping me tightly. I drink in the solitude, appreciating no longer feeling parched by the absence of distant travel. With luck I've forgotten my cell phone—this is a morning where no one can reach me as I reach closer to listening to myself. The radio is quiet—a beautiful melody of silence. The start line is full of strangers who soon seem like friends as we sweat our way up too many hills. Like brief encounters we have with other tourists while traveling, I appreciate conversation with those I likely will not see again. The drive home is even more gorgeous without racing nerves clouding my windshield.

On a weekday night I steal away to hear a friend read from her newest novel at the bookstore. I whisper and laugh with another dear friend, the two of us traveling together for the evening. One night, my husband and I find ourselves listening to music on the mall—stay-at-home tourists eavesdropping on a Texas family next to us. I wake up to a rainy morning—soft fog reminding me of the Pacific Northwest on my morning run. For a moment I play a game of make believe, far away from Boulder sunshine. So at a time when many of us forego the luxury of travel, may we remember to stay and be away, all in one beautiful week.

The Resolution of Silence

When my kids were young, we'd play a game on long car trips called the "no talking game." Who could stay quiet for the longest time? None of us were successful and quickly someone would innocently ask, "Where are the Fruit Roll-Ups?" or "Who took my shoe?" and the game was over. So when I resolved to stay quiet for ten days on a silent yoga retreat, I felt apprehensive.

When I arrived at the Meditation Center, the woman at the front desk spoke softly. "Welcome, and you do not have to worry about silence until later this evening." I was relieved I wouldn't need to use hand gestures to get oriented, as this was the first time I'd left my husband and three children, my psychotherapy practice, or my e-mail for ten days. She handed me my room key wrapped in a black cord. As I opened the door to my room, I wondered what doors would be opened by silence.

The first evening our small group met with our yoga master. We sat on mats in a warm room with beautiful music and sipped sweet tea. Our daily schedule was printed out, each day like the next, 6:00 A.M.—morning meditation, breakfast, morning session, lunch, afternoon session, dinner, evening session, 10:00 P.M.—go to bed.

I felt like a child at a camp I wasn't sure I would enjoy. The evening ended with a discussion about how daily conversations can often be distractions from honest conversations with ourselves. Quiet allows our inner voice to be heard. We were expected to be silent during the day and only speak if absolutely necessary. I wasn't sure what "absolutely necessary" meant, so I spoke up. "Excuse me, but I usually go running every morning. Would that be possible?"

"Oh, no," my master answered. "What do you run from?"

This wouldn't be a fun camp. Silence was one thing, but I had made no running resolutions.

Our first morning meditation came before sunrise—learning to walk slowly four times around the garden pond, a little different than my four-mile run. As we nodded hello under a moonlit sky, it was a relief not to make idle conversation. We breathed slowly, white wisps of cool air. We learned to focus on our feet—heel to toe, heel to toe. I soon learned that silently repeating "heal, soul, heal, soul" was calming. The silence spun a melody we actually didn't want to interrupt with conversation.

Our days continued. We held yoga poses much longer than I could imagine. We did intensive exercises to strengthen ourselves, carrying us deeper into the cradle of our souls. Often all of us flew into our heads, wondering if the Caribbean might have been a better destination. But we learned true beauty lay so near, with no need for a passport. This is the small part within us that is actually huge, holding the "soul-er" power that guides all our life decisions.

In our silence, we tried to make sense of unhealthy patterns in our lives. My back and shoulder pain was an important metaphor. Unfortunately, I've always carried a small invisible whip—always pushing myself. I was raised in a New York suburb where we stood on tiptoes reaching for wealth, achievement and beauty. I thought about the pace of life back home, where my husband and I worked long hours, took care of three children, a bounding puppy, and a spacious home. We prospered from having space in our home, yet felt deprived by no space in our lives. I drank in the simplicity of my retreat, filled by the emptiness of my appointment book.

Our small group shared a table in the dining hall. Always in silence, we were encouraged to eat mindfully, chewing our food thirty times before we swallowed. It wasn't easy and I often took bigger bites of tofu to be able to go the distance. We were the only silent table, and with each passing day the voices around us seemed louder and louder. Although everyone spoke English, it sounded foreign and so fast-paced. We could break our silence to check in with our real lives. So by mid-week the mother pull had me call home to hear about my daughter's new braces and my son's report on the latest Denver Bronco victory. The frustration of cell phone reception was a gentle reminder of the challenge of bridging these two worlds. I shared with my husband my musings about a simpler life, a smaller home, a smaller caseload, yet a larger space for passion and creativity. I struggled, feeling homesick for family and my own pillow, and homesick for what lay deeper inside me as I questioned how I wanted to live my next fifty years.

During one of the last afternoons, the gentle teacher asked, "You want to try running now?" I was both happy and scared. The challenge was "running" without "running away."

So under an Arizona blue sky, I began a meditative

run repeating, "heal, soul, heal, soul," as I had every morning. I learned much during that run. Remember to breathe. When you hit an uphill climb, lean into it and just keep going. Sometimes it's easier to go around a bush than to try plowing through. Don't make the journey more difficult; take the pebbles out of your shoes. Don't look too far ahead; you can lose your footing in the present. And as I jogged toward my room, I was reminded that in the end we all return to where we started. I had small blisters on my toes, which I learned was because my skin had softened in the contemplative desert air. My whole being had become more sensitive and open.

Speaking began with our goodbyes as we all faced the challenge of bringing quiet peace back to our red light/green light world and the loud music of our lives. We'd discovered a beautiful energy that felt like slippery soap in a morning shower—sweet smelling, but a challenge to hold.

My ten-day resolution of silence in a faraway desert was a beautiful version of the "silent game" and I returned home committed to driving my destiny versus driving myself. We decided to sell our house and move a block away to a lovely, yet simpler, home. At first the children screamed and slammed doors, but they have since forgiven us.

My husband and I work less and I spend more time writing. My husband finds peace as he tends his blossoming garden. I make time between patients to attend a daily yoga class. I dress more casually these days, cotton pants and light sweaters just so I don't have to change before and after class—my seams holding the quiet throughout the day. I drink more sweet tea than coffee, listen to quiet tunes that often compete with loud beats of teenage music behind bedroom doors.

Thus it is the bringing together of the East and the West, reconciling the junior prom limousine with the hybrid ways in the same family. When the children were young, evenings would get so wild, I'd scream something maternal like, "Can you guys just be quiet, so I can hear myself think!" How grateful I am that finally I was the one who took the time to stop talking long enough to hear.

Published in *Chicken Soup for the Soul-My Resolutions,* December 2008

Down-Sizing to Live it Up

One Friday morning began with my husband shouting, "I have no extra to give and I won't cancel a patient to take anyone to an orthodontist appointment!" After 25 years of marriage, I'm finally learning how to argue with my kind husband. Like skiing a difficult slope of moguls, confident assertiveness helps me manage the bumps. And when it's over, I hope a small bit of grace clings to my powdery anger. We're not typically a fighting, yelling couple. Perhaps in our first few years of marriage we had car ride squabbles and slamming phone hang-ups. But life is different now. When we feel we're losing it with one another, something big is happening.

As we argued about the orthodontist, we "braced" ourselves for change. With three kids between ages 14 and 21, one golden retriever puppy, two full psychotherapy caseloads and a too-big house—we were taking care of everything but ourselves. Spring had arrived and my husband was fantasizing about laying more cement, to save his back and reduce the gardening. With our eldest son away at college, I was only in the basement if I needed to fine a client file buried in the utility room. Four of us puttered comfortably in just a few rooms. Fifteen years ago when we moved into our wide-open spaced home, my four-year-old son cried, "Too much rug in this house, Mommy!"

I came to agree; there was just too much rug. The simplicity of a pretty new town home felt like the freedom of open toes in new sandals. My husband and I stopped fighting long enough to focus on how we wanted to live our next fifty years. Our schedules had no free spaces—the inverse relationship of a spacious home to no breathing room in our daily lives.

Yet I was quiet as I began to look around our home, which was a photo album of years past. The sugar cookie dough stuck between the slats of our kitchen table held tender memories. The blue and white placemats pushed to the side—my daughter's pudgy figures rolling the dough to a sticky thinness. Worn into the pale wood were tiny scratches left over from scrubbing away at Hanukah candle wax. Small stickers clung to the walls from when the children didn't know better. The Rorschach bleach spots on our bedroom rug reminded me of my son's determination in seventh grade to bleach his hair blond. Mellow white, light purple and blue walls wrapped our family like a quilt in time.

But we can't help smiling when we feel the warmth of our lovely new town home, only a block away. And as we face selling our house, our petite realtor with big demands says, "De-clutter, clean, throw away, give away, clean, de-clutter again!" I stand in my kitchen at midnight, staring at old check registers in the drawer and the purple misshapen ashtray my daughter made for her parents who never smoked. How important is the spice rack? Couldn't the basil, oregano and cinnamon join the turmeric and garlic salt in the cabinet? My cookbooks stand straight and quiet, like children who don't want to be chosen for the wrong kickball team. The toaster is in the clear, safe from the downsizing layoff. I neatly fold a pile of dishtowels and place them in a drawer; the blender joins the Cuisinart in the pantry, and I'm ready for bed.

Closets and counters are easier to organize than aligning our children to move out of their home. "Just wait until I go to college, you guys are crazy!" protests my son. "No way, I'll never stop crying!" announces my daughter as she slams her door. I begin wondering if I can live on a street named "Ralston." And my husband begins to question life without his flower garden. But with my 50th birthday next week, what better gift than a smaller home for a bigger life? And with no grass to mow, we hope to live the next 50 years a little greener.

Our Home's Shelf Life

Moving to a new home is like throwing your life up in the air and waiting up there for a couple months until everything lands in an unfamiliar kitchen. But that isn't the hard part—it's the packing of our bookshelves, the library of our lives. Heavy psychology texts from graduate school sit on a living room shelf, acting grand but long ago forgotten. Read and unread novels beckon me. *The Joy of Cooking* shares space with the *Joy of Sex* and a small copy of *Good Night Moon* reminds me of the emotional journey of sorting through my children's books.

Their books, with colorful covers and titles evoke memories of soft hands against mine, turning pages of unforgotten stories. I pull out each book, one by one deciding to keep or give away. Some I hold longer than others, remembering nights when my son would say, "Again mommy, the witch part again, pleeese." Like baby clothes long ago packed away, I hold these small worn books, startled at how fast it all went by. As individual as my children are, they learned to read at different ages and in different ways. My dyslexic son labored over *Frog and Toad*, his frustration matching my sadness that it had to be so difficult. We eventually taught him kinesthetically and I learned to read all over again, relying on a sound's feeling against my tongue. The day he read a complete sentence we went out for rainbow sprinkled donuts. My daughter effortlessly skipped through learning to read, falling asleep at night blanketed by her books, pages left open for morning. I quietly pack *Charlotte's Web* with no front cover, handed down from my own childhood.

My husband built our white bedroom bookcase soon after we moved in—giving me the gift of space to fill with all the writers who've put me to bed each night, never closing one cover until I knew I had another relationship to begin the next night. Some writers I've stayed with longer than others. I happily had one-sided conversations, where they spoke one novel at a time—delighting me when they'd publish again. I don't sort my own books—I stack them neatly, box after box, to decorate our new home.

As I look at the titles of my son's books, who is now 17 years old, I try not to be intrusive, only helpful, as I let him do his own sorting. The titles have come far from *Frog and Toad*. Instead of feeling the sounds against his tongue, he feels the power of relationships in books by Hemmingway. I spot a book of mine I'd passed on to him for one of his English classes. At times when his bedroom door remains closed more than open, knowing he's reading a book I enjoyed makes me feel we're on the same page.

Give-away books line our hallway. I feel the same discomfort as when our bunny, Lulu, moved in with the little girl down the street. But sometimes giving away is part of growing up. I found a home for abused children in need of books. Our stories will now gently put others to sleep. The books we take with us are a reminder—home is truly where our books are.

Published in the
Washington Post, April 2008

Got Neighbors?

I attended my first neighborhood meeting after moving into our new home. Not because I have major concerns about impending snow removal, cracked sidewalks, landscaping or parking. But because I want to feel part of something bigger than our high reaching town-home that stands like a child on tiptoes, stretching toward the sky. We recently moved from a neighborhood just a few blocks away where green lawns instead of rust colored stucco separated our homes; where we had mailboxes at the end of our driveway, instead of sleek silvery boxes piled one on top of the other with tiny keys for opening. I tentatively knocked on my new neighbor's door, taking a seat in the midst of neighbor introductions—a recovery group for survivors of moving, unpacking and disorientation.

"Well here's the neighborhood baker," laughed the red-haired British woman who owns a tiny black puppy always carrying a soggy tennis ball. Baking had been my way to say hello to my new neighbors without too much awkward conversation. Warm pumpkin bread softens meetings with strangers. And baking was also how I said goodbye a few weeks earlier in our old neighborhood.

On the last Sunday in our old home—with much of

my kitchen in boxes—I decided to bake cookies one last time. I had to un-tape three boxes before I found the chocolate chips and brown sugar. I blended the dough with my hands, our golden retriever by my feet taking the place of my children, who used to drag chairs over to dip their tiny fingers in dough. I don't measure sugars and flour. I do it all done by feel, matching my movements in a familiar kitchen, a fifteen-year-old dance. Hundreds of times I nestled against the counter, lost in thought, forming cookies like a child with play-dough. I shared cookies with my neighbor in a simple, old-fashioned way. Yet the true ingredients were sharing the birth of children, miscarriages, the death of parents, teenagers in trouble, ginger ale for the flu, watching our houses during vacation, and watching our children in-between. We had intimate conversations standing in the street, like "pillow talk" with our husbands. My children grew up there, and so did I. Like a college dorm, where close proximity builds family, our neighbors held us close during a grown-up's growing up.

I gingerly slid my good-bye cookies onto a small china plate and walked across the street to my dear friend and neighbor. China, not paper—for like our connection, it is daily, durable and cherished. I didn't know that when I knocked on the porch screen, what opened next would be my tears. We hugged with no words. We then took a slow walk over to our new home. We talked about the granite counter tops, pantry drawers and the knobs on our cabinets—the simplicity of just being women in a new kitchen. But I also knew I was asking for reassurance, as my son did when he tried to choose the right college campus, so ready to leave us. We moved into our neighborhood as children of an earlier decade, luckily finding kind parents in neighboring driveways. Our small community raised us to risk stepping into the next decade and a new home.

Now, as I open my new neighbor's door into a room full of smiling strangers, I realize what I'm searching for. It truly does take a village to raise all of us from one decade to the next. Neighborhoods nourish us, sweetened by friendships we share with one another.

Published in the
Denver Post, December 2007

A Family's Weave

This was the summer my husband and I moved our three kids from our "growing up" house to our "growing in" house. We wanted to downsize and live a simpler life. We sold our pool table and grill and moved two blocks away, where we settled into a reaching high town home.

Somehow in the "old house," the five of us seemed to fit together more. But in retrospect that was a bit of fantasy. There, I could always journey back in time to the more secure little children days—before a family's July 4th and the fireworks of independence. Memories were in the walls—play dough still stuck under the kitchen table, carpet stains that held a story, blanket forts always in the same place, and banister sliding. But the new house is the truth of today, without a yesterday.

I can only describe the five of us like my grocery cart. There's pepperoni frozen pizza, hot dogs, organic peaches and soymilk. We're all right next to each other, but different. When I look at my three teenagers, they all hold something in their hand my husband and I have never held. Through the walls, I hear the faint strumming of my son practicing guitar, lost in his music. I held a violin for a short time. In fifth grade I took violin lessons from Mr. Simons.

I was fascinated with the baby-like rolls of his left cheek holding the violin in place. But one day he told my mother it would be best if I gave it up. My eldest son arrives home in early evening, grass stained hands and sweaty all over, explaining his golf stroke. I've actually only been on a golf course twice. Once was lying on my back in darkness—scratchy grass and kissing my high school boyfriend. And then with my husband, running at dawn, before we were politely told to leave. My daughter clamors around our bedroom trying to perfect her cartwheel and splits, having recently begun cheerleading lessons. There were no lessons when I was young and cheerleading was reserved for popular girls who valued bosoms and boyfriends way before I was ready to put away my Keds and kickball. And then my husband and I hold yoga poses in the living room while our kids reach for the remote.

    I stand in the bookstore, lost in the titles of those who traveled across the world to find themselves, carrying only their meager belongings. They return with tales of falling in-love with strangers in cafes on cobbled streets, or loving themselves on serene mountaintops. That won't work for my husband and me: devoted to our three children, exposed to a world where the i-Phone, "juicy" clothing and prom limousines are not meager belongings. Instead, we search instead for the soul of our family when we all have different travel plans. My youngest son searches for his melody through guitar strings. My eldest son searches with discipline and focus, holding a golf club. And my daughter tries to gain mastery over a young woman's developing body. My husband and I hope for a more peaceful life with a simpler home, quieter careers, and time to listen closely to how we want to live the next 50 years. And in those moments, where by some magic, we all end up in conversation on our small front porch, I know we have found something important. It is that beautiful weave of independence, yet belonging together. And with so much time ahead of us, perhaps we'll all make it to faraway cities to fall in-love with strangers and ourselves.

Published in the
Denver Post, July 2007

Shoe and Substance Free

As a psychologist, I daily listen to adolescents talk about playing beer games and how Boulder has the best pot in the country. At night, I'm a parent who hates all of it. I listen patiently to a client describe a wild party over the weekend where the cops arrived and she had to run out the back door barefoot in the snow. She then got a ride home with Tom, who wasn't drinking because he'd already been wasted the night before. I reinforce her good decision to go home with a sober driver, then I gently confront the dangers of her behavior—a soft judgment that allows her to keep talking.

As a mother of three kids from ages 14 to 21, I have no tolerance. I cling to the idyllic hope that my children will go through high school abstinent, never experimenting. When they were toddlers we told them not to play in the street. They listened and didn't have to be hit by a car to learn. We guided them away from the oven before they were burned. Unfortunately kids don't pull away with drugs and alcohol, because they don't get burned immediately. So they're left to grapple with a philosophical issue: What feels good often isn't good for us.

Many parents say, "They're going to drink anyway, so why not let them do it safely in our home?" How can underage drinking be safe anywhere? Adolescence is a complicated, confusing time where a teenager's judgment is impaired even when sober. Adding substances to the mix seems an unsafe combination. There's the argument, "Try it in high school, so you don't go crazy in college." But maybe they don't have to try it in college either. Isn't maturity about finding a sense of peace and happiness from within—a high that's truly invaluable? I hope my kids will learn to cope with life without substances softening the blow.

I can't say I'm proud of how I handle the topic with my son, when a lighter falls from his pocket as I'm doing laundry, or his buddies inhale a plate of chocolate chip cookies at midnight. I scream, he accuses me of jumping to conclusions, we slam doors, and I feel nauseous. We eventually cool down while he stands in front of the refrigerator with the door open. He tries to reassure me with, "Don't worry Mom, I'm not a bad kid."

I try to reassure him with, "I know."

I hung a small sign by our front door where shoes of all types and sizes decorate our porch—my kids and their friends finding comfort from the cold. "Welcome To Our Shoe Free, Substance Free Home—Please Remove."

So by day, I will continue providing space for my clients to talk openly as they search for safety. By night, I'll do my best to keep guiding my own kids away from what I believe will only burn them in the end. When they make a different choice, I just set another limit, trusting they soon will learn their own limits—guiding them closer to that sense of peace we all seek.

Published in the
Chicago Tribune, April 2008

Marriage and Politics - A Cross-Examination

In keeping with tradition, for our 25th wedding anniversary my husband bought me something silver and absolutely beautiful—a sleek hybrid bicycle so I could feel the wind at my back on both trails and roads. Given we met bicycling on a far away mountain in Colorado, his gift held deep meaning. I'm a woman of the baby-boom generation, now guiding my parents through their later years. So as we celebrate our 25th I will sail on two wheels, my youngest child prepares for four, and my father sadly settles into a wheelchair.

The notion of hybrid rings with both versatility and conservation. Not only is it one of our nation's hopes for dealing with the energy crisis; it provides hope for conserving the beauty of a marriage. The very nature of a relationship begins with one half being one person, the other half a different person. From there, we conserve resources by sharing a home, a bed, earnings, parenting, cooking, dog walking and laundry (o.k. not always). This is a committed version of "carpooling."

The combination of different traits seems to actually balance and fuel our lives. When we met, he was quiet, reserved and even tempered. I talked louder, cried, laughed and worried more. Somehow over the years, we each moved more to the center. I've grown quieter and more peaceful; he seems more emotional and expressive. On a more concrete level, my husband's sparkly drum set decorates our bedroom with my meditation cushion quietly finding space near his symbols. Allowing each of us freedom of expression, cushioned by compromise, seems fundamental. So one year when I was away at a writing conference, he decided to paint the wall of the living room two complimentary colors. He painted, I wrote and we both were happy.

Tolerance and compromise energize much better than conflict. I'm not saying we don't drive each other crazy sometimes and fight about unimportant things, but in general our relationship empowers each of us to figure out how we will contribute to the greater good in this world.

With this idea of hybridism in mind, it seems important to move from the state of one's family to the state of the nation. Some criticize Obama for melting into the middle. But if we truly live in a land where we celebrate differences, versus being stymied by conflict, we need a leader who takes a political vow of compromise and tolerance without losing sight of a core commitment to integrity and the pursuit of the greater good. In simple terms, we are a hybrid nation in need of unity, versus divorce. Applying the ingredients of a good marriage to the political situation may not be so far fetched. As a psychologist, I tend to push for good communication, compromise and tolerance. And as a nation, we're in this together for the long haul; we better learn to live with each other.

My husband and I did celebrate our anniversary at a nice hotel where no one else was driving a hybrid. But I shalt not judge. And we did our best to decrease spending, as I bought my husband two beautiful silver bike pedals. We compromised, and next year he gets the fancy gift. And may we all commit to bike more, drive less and share the road with our neighbors at home and around the world.

Jail and Bail

"We don't usually do this but I'll put you directly through to the jail operator. Your voice sounds awfully nice." The police dispatcher connected me to the Boulder County Jail after-hours receptionist.

"Boulder County Jail, may I help you?"

"Yes, I was wondering if I might speak with a Rita Lester. She cleans our home and I received a collect call from the jail—I'm a little confused…"

"Well dear, we really can't allow inmates phone contact. Are you involved with the incident?"

"Incident? I was just baking brownies and the phone rang and I don't know anything about an incident."

"Well we really don't ever do this, but you sound so nice, I'll put her on the phone. But don't expect the same in the future, dear."

"No, no, I don't think I'll be calling the jail a lot."

That was how my Saturday morning began. My daughter was delighted because our cleaning lady was in jail, and it felt like her very own TV drama. Rita wasn't quite as excited as she breathlessly asked me to find a bail bondsman. The phone call was brief—just long enough to raise more questions and introduce me to an important role in this drama.

Do bail bonds people work on weekends?

I contained my daughter's excitement with a perfect mother moment. "Don't talk to me now!" I announced. Then came the yellow pages. I squinted, trying not to give in to defeat and reach for my reading glasses. To my relief, they not only had a bail bondsman listed in big print, but a 24-hour service.

I tentatively dialed, took a deep breath and hoped I was doing it right. I wasn't versed in bail etiquette.

"Bail release, this is Tammy."

"Yes, Tammy this is all new to me, but my cleaning lady is in jail..." I wasn't proud of the distance I was creating in my relationship with Rita. She'd been cleaning my home for 18 years, seen my children grow up, seen our tears after deaths, seen my diaphragm on the sink and birthday notes on the table. Announcing she was my cleaning lady came out of arrogance and shame.

"Let me walk you through this..." Tammy explained about collateral, car title, signatures and court appearances. My Saturday afternoon was beginning to look like the police drama my daughter hoped for. Tammy quickly realized I was in over my head and her voice became softer. I felt selfish as I struggled with the fact that my movie plans might conflict with Rita's release. As Tammy and I became closer friends, she finally said, "You sound so nice, I'll bail Rita out and we can put the paper work off until tomorrow."

My "nice" voice had now gotten me a direct line to the jail, a conversation with Rita and bail without collateral. We agreed on a Starbuck's meeting the following day for Tammy, Rita and me to finalize bail paperwork over lattes. I realized I was still uncertain why Rita was incarcerated, although I felt certain it wasn't theft or murder. Rita left a phone message that evening, calling me her "angel" and assuring me it was a neighbor harassment charge with no validity. My daughter was disappointed.

The following morning it took me longer than usual to get dressed, because I didn't know what to wear to meet a bail bondsperson. I chose a pink sweater. Rita arrived in a swaying black skirt and wild hair. Tammy was a small blond woman in jeans. She looked normal.

Our meeting was long, since Rita kept going off on tangents, mostly about lawsuits against the jail staff, her bank's mistakes over bounced checks, and her mother who lived in Florida who was no help to anyone. I felt sad as I watched Rita lose her footing like a runner on an icy morning. "I'm trying to slow my speech, my psychiatrist says to do that." Unfortunately she needed so much more help than slowing her speech. We all struggled with the fine print on the forms. We shared my reading glasses and for one brief moment we were all just three women bonded by aging eyesight.

Rita hugged me in the parking lot, handing me a silk shirt from a thrift store that smelled like smoke.

"Please take this, and thank-you," she said tearfully.

A New Place Named My Space

It's been a rough week for my 12-year-old daughter and me. It all began when I didn't attend her choir concert. I worked late and she actually preferred to go with friends. But I felt ashamed. Good mothers don't do that sort of thing. My shame only grew worse when she arrived home after the performance, wearing a too grown-up dress that I wouldn't have allowed her to wear. She'd left the house in a jean skirt and T-shirt embroidered with a little rainbow. Her sweetness must have been left on her friend's bedroom floor, as she wiggled into something beyond her years. I imagined the audience focusing on my daughter's dress and the poor judgement of her mother, who didn't even bother to show up.

That was Monday evening, and Tuesday I helped her with her math homework. On Wednesday, the serious sixth grade trauma began. My Space created pre-teen tears, but not because of male predators. Our daughters do just fine creating their own trauma. I'm a little confused on how one navigates through these spaces, but it seems to be an on-screen scrapbook, a colorful self-description. Or at least a description of who they think they should be, using music, pictures and quotes to enhance their image. It's a child's resume requesting a spot at the popular table. The kids post bulletins and fling criticism, the way we wrote notes and flew them in paper airplanes.

My daughter and her friends developed an on-line war that left Stephanie P. and her parents hurt and embarrassed. I had phone conversations with parents I'd never met, as my daughter cried at the kitchen table. Someone had said something about someone, who had said something at the lockers about someone else, making up terrible lies about Shephanie. Wasn't it just yesterday I held my daughter close in her tiny pink outfit, her cheek nestled against mine?

How could this happen to a child whose most risky behavior to date was eating fast food two times in a week and staying up past midnight? She was now passing devastating rumors instead of cards in Go Fish. I was a sixth grader once, and yes there were times when Susan Windsor and Lisa Hobson went home after school without me. And Andy Simons hurt my feelings when he asked for his i.d. back and then gave it to Bonnie Bryers ten minutes later. But where did my daughter and her friends learn to verbally assault one another? I thought good modeling was the core of good parenting. My parents made my childhood complicated, but they modeled values that blossomed from kindness and integrity.

Today is a different world. As a child, I bicycled freely across town where the biggest challenge was crossing one busy street. Our children's trek across town exposes them to dangers that used to be in bad neighborhoods of the inner city. Now our affluent college town is where children become dangerous to one another. They have become the fast moving delivery trucks that made my biking so scary.

It used to be my children needed me to fix broken

toys. Now my daughter was asking for help with a broken friendship. The whole group of them wanted to send an "I'm sorry" bouquet of flowers. To raise money, they had a lemonade stand and sold chocolate chip cookies door to door, pulling dozens of cookies in a red wagon. They were children seeking justice in childlike ways. But their crime had been acted out using grown-up language to spread untruths—like playing dress-up in ugly, dangerous clothing.

So I must accept that this week, I did the best I could in a world as new to me, as it is to my daughter. And once again I have learned important lessons from my children.

"Mom, don't be ashamed, then you'll teach me to be ashamed. Mom, don't lose trust, or then I'll mistrust myself. And thank you for teaching me how to say I'm sorry when I make mistakes." I may have missed a choir concert but I continue to hear the beautiful music of parenting.

Published in the
Denver Post, November 2006

Sending a Text, Without Losing the Connection

Monday through Thursday, "I chat" in "My Space." I converse with my patients in the comfort of my office, with soft green chairs, art on the wall, and a faint smell of vanilla from the candle on my desk. We "face" each other as they share their lives. But this isn't how my children experience, Facebook, I Chat, or My Space, where conversations pass from their fingertips to a computer screen and back again. They miss the crinkle of a smile, a tear, or hearing laughter. These small gestures bring warmth to the quilting of our relationships. Instead, the cool air of cyberspace wraps our children.

I have the honor of sitting with patients who share their stories without the burdening walls of technology. They teach me about their new world of communication, so I continue to have an intimate understanding of their lives—but their phones and computers are respectfully left at the door. I listen closely to a sixteen year old girl describe her recent break-up with Todd, the soccer star. "I just had to text him and say it was over."

"Could you have just spoken to him?" I ask innocently.

"No way, my thoughts get too jumbled!"

"But that is truly the way break-ups go, they are jumbly," I encourage.

"Well anyway, he responded with a private message on Facebook."

I get lost in this new way of communicating and perhaps they do as well.

My next young man, in his 20's, recounts a difficult night with his x-girlfriend. "She texted me at 3:30 a.m to say we got the house!" He went on to explain, he thought she had a new boyfriend she was moving in with. It took a few messages back and forth before he realized she was celebrating the Democrats win in the House of Representatives. He ended the session triumphantly announcing, "I'm ready to delete her number anyway!" He then flips open his phone, speed dialing and smiling goodbye at the same time.

A shy eighth grade girl weeps as she describes how sick she feels when it takes her boyfriend 15 minutes to answer her text. Her mother died when she was young and a feeling of abandonment is the only message crossing the small screen of her sequence decorated phone. My day ends with an elderly professor whose only knowledge of text are the books in his library—a small reprieve from a modern day.

With early evening, my new space becomes our kitchen—mail on the counter, afternoon snacks still opened. Since we've graduated to a T-Mobile family plan (with unlimited text messaging), I've just purchased a new, blue cell phone. Finally it isn't three times the size of everyone else's phone. My daughter is intrigued; I feel a little lost. She patiently tries to teach me to program numbers. "That's okay," I say, "I prefer to memorize."

"Mom, how about downloading a new ring tone?"

That I agree to, and she helps me choose Beethoven's Fifth. Incoming/outgoing calls, a pleasant ring tone and talking to my family for free are all I need. I like learning the basics from my daughter as much as she enjoys teaching her mother something.

We move on to discussing her book report about *A Little Princess*. Her paperback copy is losing its cover, the pages browned and thin. It is close to forty years old, found in a childhood box of mine. I help her think about classic themes as she helped me download. And I breathe easier as it all makes a little more sense to me now. I promise to be taught about the world of texting and Facebook, if I can still teach my way of connecting. So I'll continue going to my office each day where my small candle burns, and cherish conversation in the warmth of my shared space.

Cheerleading Lessons

*L*ast Sunday was gorgeous—leaves blowing and spinning in a warm breeze. I had the early morning carpool shift, driving my 14-year-old daughter and three chattering friends to the Denver Coliseum for their first cheerleading competition. I agreed to listen to their radio station with music that always sounds like someone shouting. Each girl wore make-up and hair bows perfectly placed atop slick red and blue spandex outfits—sporting white shoes without a speck or smudge of dirt. My job was to deliver them exactly two hours before they performed. I took my task seriously, since their coach warned of "serious consequences" for any athlete who arrived late. My performance was perfect as they piled out of the car seven minutes early, matching backpacks bumping their knees. I had tried to explain to a friend about this new cheerleading sport.

"You mean they don't cheer for anyone?" she asked.

"Oh no, that's a thing of the past. We now go and cheer for them!" I explained.

We've always tried to be good parents and introduce our kids to different sports, hoping one would be the magic fit. After ski lessons, tennis lessons, swim lessons, ballet lessons, basketball camps, soccer team, gymnastics, and running groups, my daughter fell in love with cheerleading. My husband and I do our best to be supportive and shield her from our clandestine conversations, where we whisper about her strict and serious coaches—skeptical about this newfound passion. There are so many rules about attendance, lateness, fees, uniforms, I'm always scared I'll be reprimanded and sent to the principal's office, even though her gym isn't affiliated with any school.

After dropping the girls off, I cherished my Sunday morning freedom before my initiation into the first competition. I found the nearest Starbucks, something familiar in this new cheerleading land. And when I paid for my tea next to a man ordering "a half calf vente three pump vanilla soy extra hot no foam latte," I smiled at being exposed to a new language during my travels.

After the pleasure of the NY Times, I made my way back to the coliseum, only making a few tourist mistakes, U-turns, driving the wrong way on a one-way street, and once asking for directions. I sat in the stands along with other parents who agreed it felt like we'd crossed the border into a new land. The girls danced in unison, did back handsprings, landed in each other's arms, did the splits, smiled widely, shot their hands in the air, and I felt proud. My snobbiness softened as my respect grew for their sweat and rigid discipline over the last few months.

But it wasn't until Sunday evening when I logged onto my computer that I was humbled by the teachings of my children. Her coaches forwarded to all the parents a recent NBC broadcast about the gym's special needs cheerleading team. I was moved by a clip of special needs young girls smiling in glory, as they performed in matching uniforms and bows. My skepticism became pride, as I realized my daughter was part of an organization that taught young girls to cheer for themselves. Perhaps this wasn't the sport I imagined for my daughter. But it reminded me our job as parents is to never disable the dreams of our children by confusing our dreams with their own.

Published in the
Denver Post, November 2007

Fear and Cheer

I made my resolution at my daughter's National Cheerleading Competition in Disney World. This was a surprising place for me to make a resolution, given Disney, cheerleading, and me are an unlikely combination. I'm usually more concerned with finding a yoga class and a pretty place to run. In contrast, my daughter had been eagerly anticipating this trip for months—training, stretching, and tumbling with the discipline of an Olympian. "And the rides Mom, now that will be great!"

Great wasn't the first word that came to mind when I thought about roller coasters in the dark and elevators crashing from the sky. But that kid-like sparkle in her brown eyes made me reconsider. I'd always been terrified of scary rides—safely watching, holding my children's melting ice cream as they danced in the sky high above. Their laughter and excitement were a joy to watch, but sharing it would be even better. So as my daughter hoped to return with a national award, I wanted to return having championed my fear. She was training to do flips in the air and I was preparing to fly—holding on for dear life.

All cheerleaders had to be accompanied by a parent chaperone, and compared to my husband,

I'm a pom-pom professional. We attended numerous meetings with coaches where we received lists, competition schedules, bus schedules, lodging specifics, and rule sheets as we prepared for the launch of two hundred cheerleaders. I'd do my best to be a good cheerleading mom, but I also knew I was going to lead a silent cheer for myself that wasn't written on any of the handouts.

I tried to be organized for our adventure, buying my Disney ticket on-line. Unfortunately I proudly purchased a three-day pass to Disneyland in California instead of Disney World in Florida. The smiley woman at guest relations shook her head, apologized, and politely handed it back to me. "Y'all will just have to buy a new $250 pass." And then... "All righty, I'll give you a complimentary ticket, but shush now and just keep yourselves movin'." Her small gesture was like a fortune cookie message, "Resolutions can cost nothing, but be worth everything." She suddenly looked enchanting and the Magic Kingdom—just magical.

We spent the weekend in a "clump"—four daughters and four mothers, busing it between competitions. My daughter lives her fourteen-year-old life in a clump, a group project with her friends, devoted to growing up all too quickly. In contrast I have dear friends, but have always appreciated my solitude. Group travel isn't usually my chosen mode of transportation. So along with roller coasters and elevators that drop from the sky, I was confronting my shyness in a group of moms, among an even larger group of tourists, bumping elbows, all searching for the electrifying thrill of Disney.

Since it was a freezing weekend in Orlando, I did have to purchase two pairs of Mickey socks to wear with my sandals, which got a few looks from my daughter. But she often finds me embarrassing these days; Mickey socks are the least of it.

The true warmth came from spending time with the other mothers. Quickly, we stopped talking about the weather and began sharing our lives, loves, losses, heartaches and laughter. They were patient with me, as I tend to ask curious questions both in and out of my psychotherapy office. My mother always reminds me that at age four I asked a divorced neighbor, "Exactly what didn't you like about your first husband?" Trailing behind four adolescent jabbering girls with large red and blue bows in their hair was contagious. We mothers began to wonder if we'd soon be texting each other, sipping from the same straw and borrowing clothes.

Given that the girls spend much of their lives "getting ready," we all found ourselves stumbling toward our toothbrushes at 5:30 A.M.—preparing for the 7:00 bus launch, with the coach refrain in our head, "DON'T EVER, EVER BE LATE!" With the end of the competition, the girls made us all proud. But for me, the biggest challenge was just beginning. We all "clumped" together to plan our afternoon rides. I found myself saying, "You know I could always sit with a cup of tea and my book." My new friends laughed, letting me know there was no back door at Disney.

I'd already decided I would need a way to manage my anxiety. I began to think of those moments in yoga class when the soft voice of my teacher guides us through a meditation. I find that place inside where for a moment the world is truly peaceful. I asked my daughter if she'd sit next to me on the elevator ride that drops from the sky. How many nights had she come running in, in the dark, whispering, "Mommy, I'm scared." And now it is my turn to rely on my grown-up daughter. We buckled up laughing and screaming before the ride even began. I tried to breathe in and out and find that yoga place, depending on both myself and my small community to keep me safe. And suddenly WHOOOOSH! We were dropping, shrieking and holding each other tight.

The exhilaration left me tearful and with that childlike feeling of "Again Mommy, again."

Of course, we did celebrate with another time high in the sky. But the true celebration was getting on board with dear friends and "clumping it." I learned to rely on strangers who had become friends, reminding me that group travel provides a smoother ride in this wild and spinning world. One resolution has led me to another, which is to risk leaning on others more, because it gives us all the chance to fly. And that is something we can cheer for.

Published in
Chicken Soup for the Soul-Resolutions, December 2008

Room for Cream?

*I*t is noon on Wednesday. I greet my afternoon patient as I have for the past five years. This appointment is a quiet reservation she has with me, rarely missed. She is pale and thin, wearing a delicate white blouse, loosely open below her neck. I see a hint of her bandage, which begins the story of what she has bravely endured over the past year. She has undergone multiple surgeries to remove malignant tumors that keep appearing like weeds on a green lawn and resist even the most dangerous of sprays. She hands me a grocery sack brimming with vegetables from her garden. The bag is heavy and she sighs as she passes it to me, relieved to have help with her burden.

She carefully sits down and begins, "I'm just so tired." She explains how her six-year-old son started first grade that day, his first full day of school. Her three-year-old daughter is excited about pre-school, which will begin the following week and her baby has graduated to only one nap a day. I think of my oldest son leaving for college, already having had many "full" school days. My patient and I have had a strong connection over the years, as we are both mothers of three children. Her plight is painful for both of us as we face serious illness while wearing a mother's apron.

It began nine months ago with a brief phone message. "Hi, it's Jan. Could you give me a call?" She had to cancel her Wednesday appointment—she needed to have a "funny feeling" lymph node checked out. Her physician decided to remove it. "Nothing to worry about, but we should probably have a look at it." That was sometime after Thanksgiving and by Christmas the "nothing to worry about" turned into radiation and chemotherapy.

Our sessions focused on how sick she felt, both from fear and chemotherapy. "My baby is too young to remember me if I go... and who will write the Christmas cards?"

I thought about going on-line to research lymphoma. But the medical specifics were less important than the specifics of her personal and tender grip on life, praying for the chance to read *Good Night Moon* until her kids were too old to listen.

She endured repeated tests. Tests used to refer to memorizing spelling words and state capitols— Dover, Delaware; Albany, New York. But for the tests she was taking, you can't prepare and the grade becomes gradation and prognosis. She explained how the cancer had traveled to the bones in her sternum. The previous year, she smiled about her son's charting Santa's sleigh, one home to the next. We were now charting this dark visitor bearing a mother's worst fear.

Winter soon became spring, and then summer. As her children blossomed, her body weakened. And now, as her son loads his school backpack, she's packing a small suitcase for a bone-marrow transplant. "They say I should bring my computer and books, comfortable pajamas and my will." She weeps as she wonders which child she will hug last.

Her parents will care for them, as she must be away for six weeks. Her husband will be with her during her long labor, as he was with all her children.

This is our last session before she leaves. I remind her of the pretty blue mug she gave me at Christmas time. I tell her the ceramic handle has a beautiful way of keeping your hand warm. I want her to hold onto it until we meet again. My tears soften my gift. She tells me how when she'd stop for coffee before she got sick, the same pretty lady with flowing blond hair would ask, "Room for cream?" My patient reminds me, "We need to say yes more." I hug her goodbye.

As my son packs for college, I wrap up a few pieces of zucchini bread I baked from my patient's gift of vegetables.

"Take it for the road," I say.

"No thanks, Mom."

I hand it to him and smile, " Why don't you let me take care of you for as long as I can?"

My words are the silent wish of another mother I know.

Published in the
Denver Post, October 2007

Crimes of Ignorance

One late afternoon, I returned a phone call from a woman requesting couple's therapy. "I don't routinely see couples but I'd be happy to give you names of therapists who could be helpful," I offered.

She was appreciative and answered, "Thank you, and if you could, perhaps not a New York City Jew."

I'm a Jew. I didn't go to temple as a child, learn Hebrew, have a bas-mitzvah, or marry a Jew. But I wear it like an invisible prayer shawl, wrapping me in permanence. Both my parents are Jews; my father grew up in Detroit, eating Kosher and wasn't allowed to turn lights on on the Sabbath. My mother was a New York City Jew who celebrated Hanukah and Christmas. My siblings and I were raised not going to temple, but reading psalms on Sunday morning. We held small *red* leather books and would sit in our living room reading aloud. We lit Hanukah candles, hung Christmas cookies on our tree, and strung popcorn. No matter how confusing it may look on the outside, I am as clear about being a Jew as I am about being a woman. But today I remain as confused and shocked by anti-Semitism as I did as a child.

We were the only Jews in our neighborhood and I thought that was part of being Jewish—Jews were different. That felt comfortable until I was old enough to know better. My friends told me Hanukah was invented for Jewish children who didn't celebrate Christmas. They told me I couldn't be Jewish, "Because you're nice." I remember my mother's words when I asked to watch the fireworks at the Bedford Country Club.

"Honey, you know they don't allow Jews as members." The fireworks lost their sparkle. Later that summer I competed in tennis on their pristine clay courts. I was frightened they might notice my curly Jewish hair and ask me to leave. My mother didn't come and watch that match. She said she had a dentist appointment, but I don't think so.

We never used the word anti-Semitism, not in Westchester in the 1960's. We traveled a lot, but we never went to Germany or bought a Volkswagen. We clung to our own prejudices just as our neighbors held onto theirs.

I never knew where the temple was in our town. Our Brownie troop met at the Presbyterian Church; I attended a pre-school at the Unitarian Church; I had piano lessons at the First Congregational Church. Churches were activity centers with that "library quiet" and hard floors. Sometimes I'd go to Catholic Church with Carrie Callaci. We'd wear Kleenex on our small heads. I just did what I was told, but again was frightened I'd be asked to leave. Because my father's side remained more religious, we always attended the bar mitzvahs of my Detroit cousins. I loved the feel of my dad's black shiny yamiaka he kept in his sock drawer. He'd pull it out for these special occasions and I'd proudly sit next to him as he read Hebrew as easily as I read Nancy Drew mysteries. It was there I belonged.

And decades later as I hold the receiver to my ear,

I am as appalled at myself as I was at this stranger. I gave her two names of Denver area therapists and hung up the phone. Religious differences have disrupted world peace for centuries, and shamefully my avoidance of that truth for only a moment made me a contributor to continued conflict. For that stranger will perpetrate again.

I apologize to myself, to all Jews, and to all minorities for ignoring ignorance late one Thursday afternoon. I help individuals remember so not to repeat sorrow and hardship. As long as I remember a child's fear on a faraway tennis court, my voice will never again be silenced by those less educated.

Published in the
Denver Post, August 2007

A Daughter's Toast to a Father's Bagel

"Four sesame, two poppy in a plastic bag if I could?" I say to the nice man with a pierced ear behind the bagel counter. Bagels have seasoned my nutritional and emotional world since I can remember. My father's bagel, butter, bacon sandwiches dripped a salty sweetness on Sunday mornings. The richness matched his warm love that started from his sloppy blue leather slippers and spread to the top of his peppery gray hair. He enjoyed making me these breakfast sandwiches as much as I enjoyed eating them. We could only eat one kind of bagel: New York City's H&H. He'd pick up half a dozen every few days. Never more—you can't eat a bagel that's not fresh. We weren't big on cream cheese, unless it was cream cheese and olive sandwiches on Jewish rye. But H&H bagels only needed butter, spread when the bagel was still hot so my father's fingers jumped a little as he called, "Bagel's done!"

When I was 16 years old, my parents were divorced and my dad moved out. I stopped eating bagel, butter, and bacon sandwiches—among other things. Bagels remained however. My father continued bringing home the bagels to a different house and eventually a different wife. The bagels were always there when I visited; he'd toast them just right. I only ate one half, and always plain. I'd seen a friend dip her bagel in tea. I tried it, thinking of Oreos in milk, donuts dipped in coffee. But I only needed to do that one time; a soggy, wet bagel was far from my heritage. My bagel was spread with an adolescent resentment that lessened when I went off to college.

Once a week, the large padded manila envelope arrived, stuffed with bagels—poppy and sesame seeds sprinkling into our dorm room. I shared more than I ate, but the smell made me feel at home. At age 19, I bicycled 4200 miles across the country. The ten mail stops along the way brought ten bagel packages. From Independence, Missouri to Reedsport, Oregon, my father never missed a bagel delivery.

When I transferred from upstate New York to a Colorado college, not only did the bagels have to travel farther, but I was in a town that hadn't heard of bagels. A breakfast round with a hole in the center was a "donut" in Boulder, Colorado. Now the bagels arrived by Federal Express to keep their freshness. When I fell in love and moved in with the man who is now my husband of 25 years, he'd smile when the Federal Express truck arrived. "The bagel truck is here!" he'd call. He loved to spread cream cheese on his bagel and add a slice of ham. When I was pregnant with the first of our three children, my butter came back—and lots of it.

Now came the question of religion and how we'd raise our children. My husband, being Catholic and myself a Jew, called for a compromise. We agreed to raise the children meditating, eating bagels and celebrating Hanukkah and Christmas. My son's first solid food was tiny bagel pieces broken from my morning bagel. As a toddler, I took him to the first bagel shop that opened. He was verbal enough to say, "Papa Mike bagel better." I had to agree. With the birth of my second son came "Moe's Broadway Bagel," and finally they had found the magic.

On a Friday evening in winter, I had to tell my father the truth. "Dad I think... I think we found a good bagel out here." We were both quiet and I knew I needed to say more.

"Dad, I really don't think you need to keep sending them." I hesitated and added, "Or maybe, just not as frequently."

My father quietly answered, "Oh."

Like breaking the Sabbath bread, our bagel bond was broken that Friday evening. I knew I had to be the adult and reassure my 70-year-old father this didn't mean I didn't love him. We both laughed at how silly it felt to make such a big deal about bagels. But we also knew our years of feeling were spread thick atop those sesame and poppy seed bagels.

My children now connect with me through bagels. A "mommy" bagel is ever so slightly toasted and spread with butter, never margarine. As each child entered adolescence, there have been shouts of, "Isn't there something DIFFERENT for breakfast than bagels!"

My oldest son now attends college in Florida. No bagel deliveries are necessary. But when he flew in for the holidays late one night, I did make him a "mommy" bagel toasted just right. I can only hope he tastes the sweet warmth I felt as my father's daughter.

Published in the
Boulder Camera, January 2007

Tasting Forgiveness

I first met my stepmother on a sandy beach in Martha's Vineyard when I was sixteen years old. Really, we'd already met—actually many times before—as she'd been my dad's new wife for a few months by then. I just hadn't faced it until I stood next to her, in her bright orange bathing suit and wide-brimmed hat. Comparing her flat stomach and my adolescent tummy made it real. This was the stomach my father had chosen over mine. So for the month of August, I ate small pieces of salmon next to tiny trees of broccoli, drank lots of iced tea, and ran on the beach, sweat dappling my brown curls—a poor substitute for buried tears.

Before that summer I'd always loved the Vineyard, where for one month my parents, sister, brother, and I vacationed. We left the busy, confusing life of the New York City suburbs, where my father spent his life on the commuter train, my mother at her keyboard, and my older sister and brother in their field hockey, lacrosse, aftershave and lip gloss worlds. I carried a red rubber ball, played kickball for hours, and wondered what it would be like to have one of those families where everyone wasn't so smart and there wasn't any yelling.

On the Vineyard, my family was more like the one

I imagined. My father wore sloppy shoes and khakis with buttery stains from corn on the cob. We rented an old home with dusty books on the bookshelves and stacks of poker chips as bookends. I learned to play poker with pennies we found at the bottom of my mother's purse and in my father's sock drawer. My parents played—my mother laughing at my father's jokes, and I'd catch a wisp of love between them. We played family tennis and I was allowed to rotate in, only knowing how to bounce the ball in front of me to serve. No one seemed to care, as competition was left behind, hidden in the towering trees of the suburbs. I was never scared at night, believing bad things didn't happen to children on vacation. And I'd awake to the smell of toasting bagels. It was okay to have sandy feet all the time and I learned to catch ocean waves, the salty thrill of creating your own ride.

But then it all changed—my parents divorced at a time when having a mom's house and a dad's house wasn't what everyone did. My brother and sister were away at college, so my mother, golden retriever, and I watched my father pack his belongings in big brown leather suitcases. I wondered if there was a way to keep it all secret, so my friends would never know. My father rented an apartment in the city that smelled like boiled potatoes, with sparse kitchen counters that made it look like no one lived there.

Soon my Dad started wearing pressed khaki pants and yellow Lacoste shirts. He introduced me to his new friend, who had three children of her own. Then we were all standing around her kidney-shaped swimming pool watching them get married. My father kissed another woman as lamb barbecued on a fancy grill. We all blended together like polite cousins. At first, my stepmother was a distant aunt who introduced me to Bloomingdale's and taught me how to make a piecrust—kneading the dough until it was soft. But it wasn't until that first trip to the Vineyard that I realized she was there to stay. I buried my adolescent grief with every spoonful of food I turned away. I tried to learn the back and forth dance from my mom's house to my dad's house, but I tripped a lot.

After visiting my dad, I'd walk into our quiet new home, for just my mom and me. Instead of feeling the pain, I would feel the cold iron of our heavy black scale, sitting in judgment. I pulled my sweater and shirt off together over my head, my underwear tucked in my pants on the floor. I put my watch on the bathroom counter. Then I'd pee, flush the toilet, and gingerly step onto the black rubber, lining my feet up perfectly. The numbers would spin high and then settle low, matching my slowing heartbeat. One more time, I would step off and on again for good luck. I would breathe and relax, my ritual completed for that afternoon. The soft yellow blanket I carried as a little girl had been replaced by the sound of the scale's heavy metal—tricking me into believing safety and security were wrapped in my thinness.

As a college freshman, I spent my time running through snowdrifts, reading French novels, eating cottage cheese, and chatting with my friends. But one day, the tone of our conversation changed as I sat pushing lettuce around my plate. "You know—it doesn't have to be this hard," my friend said.

I knew she was right, and I made my way to the counseling office, where a woman with sparkly eyes said, "Here, take a seat. Do you want to talk?"

I started crying and my healing began. There were so many feelings buried under my baggie sweatshirt. At first I was ashamed I needed help—afraid of people thinking I was crazy. But I slowly learned to change my humiliation into humility. My therapist helped me talk about my feelings instead of swallowing them. One day, I put my scale in a brown garbage bag and threw it away in a nearby Dumpster. I learned to find nurturance in my relationships, wrapped by the security of friendships instead of harsh numbers on a scale. I always thought I needed to forgive the grown-ups in my life who had turned my world upside down. But it wasn't them I needed to forgive. Instead, it was me—the young girl with a small, soft stomach, who believed if I had been good enough, thin enough, strong enough, I could have kept my parents together.

It's amazing the lies we tell ourselves. Someday I'll go back to that beach just to be reminded of the salty, yet beautiful taste of forgiveness.

> Published in *Chicken Soup for the Soul: Teens Talk High School,* November 2008

An Iron Mother

The fitness room at the Ft. Lauderdale Holiday Inn has two treadmills, one loud stair-master, two stationary bikes, neatly rolled white towels by the door, and a commanding doctor's scale. As I spin and sweat on the bike, the smiling woman next to me steps off the treadmill with relief. Ten minutes later she arrives back, this time in her bathing suit to use the scale. The least amount of clothing is obviously important. She rushes out as a blond woman in spandex dashes in, "Just checking my weight!" she apologizes to me as if she needs to explain why she's coming and going so quickly.

A woman's relationship with the scale is complicated. I no longer own one and haven't had one in our home for twenty years. When my son was little he stretched out a tape measure and asked, "Mommy, I know you never like to know how much you weigh, is it the same for how tall you are?" But over the years, my children have come to better understand why I needed a clean break.

I began my affair at sixteen with an iron gray scale in my mother's bathroom. It was rusty, cold, and very powerful in my world. It was how I coped, how I cried, how I survived my parent's divorce.

My parents fought for years and I managed to stay

afloat. But when they divorced, the scale slowly began to manage me.

She was someone I trusted; she was always there, and her message was solid and clear, with no emotion. I could come and go and she'd be there when I returned, comforting me in being thin. All too soon, I was controlled and abused by this iron mother who wouldn't let go. A pound more and her imagined criticism made me feel sad, mad, and anxious. A pound less—I was her proud and confident daughter. Like a play director, she demanded and controlled my expression and feeling —a voice that wasn't my own.

The "she" scales have decorated the bathrooms of my past for years. I was a young woman ruled by numbers. But recovery from an eating disorder brought me the truth about my iron perpetrator. She became just pliable metal and I was the sculptor with the power to do with her what I must. So one blue-sky morning in Colorado, I buried her in a Safeway Dumpster, which seemed an appropriate farewell.

I know many woman can use scales in a healthy way to monitor their physical health and well-being. I am not one of them. It isn't easy to be our own, scale weighing in with our emotions and assessing our bodies by how we feel on the inside. But that's is a better life raft than clinging to something so heavy it could sink me in the end.

Sometimes I wonder if my children feel deprived about growing up without a scale. But the health of the real mother does seem more important. So, for now, I prefer to walk on past the ominous creature, celebrating life free from her grasp and appreciating the challenge of finding my own internal balance. And in answer to my young son many years ago, "Sure you can measure how tall I am, but the truth is we never stop growing on the inside, so we'll have to find a really big tape measure!"

Published in the
Boulder Camera, February 2009

My Grandfather's Paper Trail

My grandfather owned a paper company, so I grew up with all the paper I wanted. I never saw the fancy paper. But we had stacks of off-white paper, so I could color endless reams of pictures, with a big green stripe across the bottom and blue stripe across the top. My crayons were all sizes, thick and thin—their paper unraveling between my tiny fingers. Soon I learned to write stories and became the author and illustrator of my first series, "Billy Leaf Adventures." Proudly I'd cut and staple these books made from my grandfather's paper.

Summer Saturdays were spent at my grandparent's house. They had a swimming pool where all the kids learned to swim, dive and listen to my grandfather's raspy voice tell us stories. My grandmother was the only one who never learned to swim. She'd float in a big black inner tube, tolerating the splashing around her.

My grandfather smoked cigars as big as I was. Sometimes he'd just chew on the end until the next bee sting. Bees loved my grandparent's house as much as we did. When the sting happened, we'd run crying to my grandfather. He'd chew off enough tobacco to spread on the red wound—a warm tobacco kiss. Sometimes I noticed him sitting, lost in thought, and scribbling on a pad of paper. My mother always said, "Oh he's just writing ideas for his company column." I liked the sound of company column—it almost rhymed.

Our lunchtime meal was always the same, steak grilled on an outdoor brick oven. My grandfather, still clad in swim trucks, would grip a wire handle that held the steaks flat between a bottom and top grill—juice dripping into the fire below. He was the boss of the bees, the meal, and all of us. He'd sit at the end of the table on their screened porch always saying the same thing, "Now isn't that the best steak?"

We'd drink small bottles of 7-Up as the grownups cut our steak, neatly arranged next to peas and potatoes from a can. And then the waiting began, exactly one hour before we could swim again. If you didn't wait a full hour after eating, you would get a cramp and drown. I'd pass the time in the kitchen with Noni, who had the most beautiful black skin I'd ever seen. Her wrinkles matched the wrinkles of her stockings down around her knees. Wrinkles that folded me up secure and warm. I liked to show Noni my "Billy Leaf" stories. She couldn't read, so I'd sit close to her on a metal stool, reading out loud. I'd leave her with some books, so at least she could look at the pictures. And then I'd head back to the pool where my brother, sister and cousins were dangling their toes in the water. The frequent question, "How much longer?" became its own melody.

Winter Saturdays were different. Visits to my grandparent's house came scrunched in the back seat of their big black Cadillac. The smell was a mixture of gray leather seats and their driver, Ozzie's aftershave. I loved to look at the back of his neck stretching up to his black cap. We were off to a Saturday in the city, and FAO Schwartz replaced the swimming pool.

Lox and bagels and bingo games filled the afternoon. I wrote a "Billy Leaf" story about wind blowing in the country and the city.

Soon my grandfather stayed sitting longer and began using a cane to lift himself out of his cushioned chair. He'd beckon us over to share a butterscotch from his deep pocket. We never really needed it—there were candy dishes all over the apartment, but from his pocket it was special. Sometimes he'd hand me a pad of paper and say, "Write something, honey."

One January morning, he died in the ambulance on the way to the hospital. My grandmother said he was furious; he wasn't ready to stop sitting at the head of the table or healing bee stings. I always wondered if he died with a pad of paper in his pocket.

My columns are my thank you notes to my grandfather, with unseen tobacco stains in the corner.

A Jury of One's Peers

Jury duty is a beauty pageant in reverse. You're asked questions about yourself that you try to answer intelligently and honestly, and then hope they don't pick you. My first day began at 8:00 A.M. at the Boulder County Courthouse.

Passing through security with my backpack—the woman, wearing snug blue pants, belted just below large breasts, smiled at the fruit on the screen. "Well dear, you'll have plenty of healthy snacks," she laughed. I didn't need snacks though; I was just stopping in for an hour. I found my way to the heavy doors labeled Jury Selection and selected a seat among other prospective jurors with open laptops, heavy novels and magazines. I had my appointment book and fruit. I was not a prepared juror. The excitement grew when a proper gray haired woman in a proper green suit asked us to file quietly to a courtroom down the hall. Things were getting serious and my morning was beginning to feel a little disrupted.

We sat down in the courtroom only to rise again when the woman judge arrived. As a Jew in church, I had learned to follow the ups and downs, so not to get in any trouble. She was kind and smiled, thanking us for our participation and encouraging us to use the lavatory. We wouldn't be able to leave the courtroom once jury selection began. Wisely, I cancelled my 9:00 and 10:00 patients.

The judge continued to smile and explain what we could expect during the next few hours. The gold plated sign in front of her neatly folded hands, read, "Care" as her first name. Could her name really be "Care?" Momentarily distracted by her name, I missed the direction to raise our right hands and solemnly swear. Quickly I imitated the others.

The judge read the names of 12 of us, randomly chosen. Unfortunately I was a semi-finalist. We were introduced to the defense lawyer, the defendant, and the prosecutor. The defendant wore too much blue, but looked harmless. His lawyer looked uncomfortable in a gray suit with a vest and slick hair. I was wearing Teva sandals, with my hair still damp from a hurried shower. The woman lawyer on the other team also wore an uncomfortable suit, pantyhose and pumps. I wondered if they liked their jobs. The air-conditioning was too high and I wanted a bagel.

How we answered a series of ten questions would help decide the final winning jury group. In accordance with her name, the judge gently asked prying questions.

"Have you or anyone close to you been convicted of a crime?"

"What is the occupation of you, your parents, spouse, and children?"

"Have you ever been hospitalized for a mental illness?"

"Is anyone blind or deaf?"

An older woman in front of me revealed she'd been jailed for trespassing at an anti-nuclear rally. She'd also been sued by her first husband for ignoring a restraining order and her parents were both dead, but had owned a bakery in Ohio. The man next to her was still healing from a bar fight where he'd been hit by a pool cue. Assault charges were pending. A young woman in her twenties was married to a Safeway manager and had gotten two speeding tickets when she was 16 years old.

My turn grew closer and I was practicing my answers in my head, when the judge said, "I know you. You compete against me in running and always win." She told me she hadn't been racing recently because of a knee injury. She went on to let everyone know I was an excellent runner and she'd loved my recent essay in the local paper. I thought we were getting off track, but didn't think it was my job to redirect things. People smiled politely, except for the pool cue man, who seemed to be growing impatient. I began to answer the ten questions, explaining my father still worked as a TV executive at 85 years old and my mother was a journalist. I omitted the most recent speeding ticket I'd gotten on the way to my daughter's soccer game.

A few more stories were told and we finished with the librarian whose elderly cousin had been killed by a drunk driver. She tearfully revealed if the case was in anyway related to driving charges under the influence, she couldn't be an unbiased juror. The judge kindly excused her and I handed her a Kleenex on her way out the door.

Finally the lawyers stopped flipping through their legal pads and the votes were tallied. They'd chosen six jury finalists who would give their clients a fair trial. My name wasn't called and I was strangely disappointed. The truth was, the whole morning had begun to feel like a getting to know you tea party without the cups of tea. Our hostess was a kind woman in a long black dress. We'd listened to one another's stories compassionately, and politely let our hostess ask the questions. As I hurried to my car I thought about them all eating sack lunches on the lawn without me. I never did know what the case was about. But the stories I witnessed were the important voices that morning in a courtroom with a judge named "Care" presiding.

Published in the
Boulder Camera, September 2007

Hospital Country

Hospitals are cold. You need socks in summer and a sweater all the time. I was new in this foreign country, hospital country. I knew mountain standard time, east and west coast time, but hospitals have their own clocks. There really are no minutes, just hours. It can be 9:00 AM and then noon very quickly when you're waiting as I was.

They had found a mass on the lining of my mother's 79 year old stomach. She didn't tell me it was the size of a baseball until we were in the taxi on the way to the hospital. "Now don't make that face honey. There really is nothing to worry about," my mother assured me, absently patting my hand.

Her surgery was scheduled for 10:00 AM.; we had two hours of pre-operation steps—a complicated operation in itself. A pile of large green folders awaited us at the curved front desk guarded by two large women; gatekeepers to this unknown country. My mother read the "Washington Post" while I tried to read the faces of those around me. No one looked sick; old maybe, but not sick. Their privacy was well guarded. No one knew their inside stories. Only the colored bands on their wrists revealed what team they were on. My mother's was orange, with a white band that read "Penc," alerting everyone she was allergic to penicillin. How did I never know that?

"Roberts, Ladley, Stafford!" bellowed a woman with white shoes and a blue lab coat. Mr. Roberts, Ms. Ladley and Ms. Stafford tentatively rose from their seats and in single file followed the blue coated woman. I thought of the WWII showers, unsuspecting Jews led to their deaths. "Dann, Lester, Romiro!" My mother stood in line. I was told I could see her after the "gowning."

I soon joined her in a curtained area next to the coughing lady my mother was convinced would make us all ill. After about an hour (there really are no minutes, it simplifies things when everything else seems so complicated) we heard the coughing lady told she was too ill for surgery. "I could have told them that, for goodness sakes," chimed my mother. "Silliness to have her here." Our conversation wove along as my mother reminded me of her lawyer's name. Now and then she'd ask if all this was "really necessary" and wondered if we could just "skip the whole deal."

"If anything happens to me, you don't have to have a memorial right away, and I'd like Chopin Mazurkas played at my funeral. Vicky can play the piano." I had never heard of Vicky. Suddenly I had a whiff of sadness I describe as this "mommy" sadness—a touch of being a little girl again, wanting her mommy. Just like my ten year old daughter on the phone last night, "Mommy, do you think you could come home now? I want you to."

So many lab coats wandered in and out. Many wore either rubber or leather clogs, obviously more cool than the white shoes with squeaky soles. Everyone smiled and asked specific intrusive questions about my mother's stomach. I'd never thought much about her stomach beyond the superficial fat or thin, which seemed unimportant now. One group of clogs would leave, and then more would come. It was a teaching hospital so everyone walked in pairs, talking teacher, attending student.

"It's time to go, Ms. Dann, and you're going to be just fine." This from was one of the smiley interviewers I found extra soothing. You see, hospitals aren't cold in that way; it's just the weather. I kissed my mom's cheek as I do with my own children, assuring them no need to be scared, morning will be here soon.

I walked out to the waiting room to greet my mother's oldest friend who I hadn't seen since I was a child. Her smile and sparkly eyes were the same, with one or two more wrinkles. I sank into her hug, teary and for the first time scared in this foreign land where I didn't understand the language. Strangers were in charge and things could be dangerous. We talked over tea about the last forty years, comforted by what we knew had happened in contrast to not knowing what was going to happen. Sometimes I would crumble in the middle of a story and ask, "Is she going to be okay?"

Barbara would answer, "Of course dear, that mother of yours is so strong."

The whole morning had been trading off the baton of comfort. My mother to me, me to her, medical people in clogs to her, my siblings' cell phones to my cell phone. Yet every once in a while the comfort baton was lost and no one could find it, and we just had to live with the truth about everyone dying someday.

Every now and then the huge metal doors to the surgery corridor opened wide like a curtain signaling the second act. Doctors or coated people made an entrance. I was only interested in seeing Dr. Lin, the surgeon who was king of this new land. He held so much power I both feared and revered him. Strange, considering we'd only met a few hours ago and had spoken with for six minutes.

By this time two more of my mother's friends had arrived. Peter sat quietly with pen and paper. "You have to write everything down or you forget what they say." I would later learn he was right. Details get lost when you're listening to medical information about someone you love.

Dr. Lin finally did appear. I kept staring at his hands as he spoke, searching for something of my mother, yet frightened I might see blood somewhere. He described the tumor as the size and shape of a lemon. I imagined the baseball now had two points to it. They were able to remove all of it, but the biopsy findings wouldn't be available for a week. He had a way of communicating clearly, without confusion, so we were all left with as solid an "I don't know" as humanly possible.

Act II was my mother post-op. The show must go on and with grace my mother lay in ICU with tubes we could see and tubes we could not. Bags of fluids surrounded her, going in and coming out. She spoke through parched lips, quietly affirming, "I don't want to complain, but this is AWFUL."

We began the sitting, comforting my mom indirectly by our murmuring among ourselves. I had grown closer to Barbara and Peter hour by hour. My mother's vulnerability was the key that freed us from the reserve of our private worlds. The nurses came and went, caretaking our small tribe. Now and then my mother would apologize for putting all of us through this. We'd smile, holding our secret that we all felt healed by the love contained in her curtained room.

I am now flying home from that foreign land. The

baton has been passed to my sister, to pass among my new friends, doctors, nurses and my healing mother. Really, we must all travel to that foreign land. There is so much to learn. If you bring a sweater, socks and a good friend, you will do just fine.

Lights Out

"I think the Christmas tree was dryer than usual this year," my husband shouts from the living room. Pliers in hand, he turns the stand's rusty screws—each turn taking us farther from the ribbons and celebration of the day before.

Like life, it was a Christmas with a bit of everything. A beautiful snow brought magic, but also the white surrender of my stepmother's battle with cancer. Like when the electricity went out Thanksgiving Day, the lights also went out on our Christmas. Within 24 hours we went from slippers and sweaters, I-pods and pie to a family traveling like the maps in the airline seat pockets—each line taking us in different directions. My son had to return to college in Florida; my other son headed up to the mountains with our puppy in tow; my daughter was farmed out to close friends, and my husband and I packed somber outfits for a NYC funeral, where they always seem to wear black anyway.

My 85-year-old father has been married for close to 60 years—23 years to my mother and 36 years to my stepmother. I walked my father slowly down the isle after her casket, grieving the end of an era for all of us. Just as slowly, we drove in black cars of the funeral procession, the conversation a jumble of non-sequiturs. Our rabbi was interested in where my brother had purchased his retro sunglasses? My father kept telling the driver he was not taking the most direct route out of the city—searching for some control in a life stage where he had none. My daughter called on my cell phone asking if eight friends could hang out at our house, even if we weren't home, and I was inquiring about Tylenol given the immediate development of a headache.

As we each traditionally threw dirt on the casket, my father crumpled in my arms.

He's a man who still goes to the office—a highly successful executive who watches the news and stock market carefully, along with writing his book. But it isn't the big things I worry about; he handles those well. It was watching him answer the door in his underwear in the morning and pouring the coffee grounds into the compartment for water that concerned me. Arriving at their home after the burial was a mixture of turkey sandwiches and conversation with people I hadn't seen since I wore Ked sneakers and carried around a red kick-ball. I watched my father nod, smile and cry—at times obviously puzzled by who he was shaking hands with.

Names, faces, coffee makers and shirt buttons seem to be his biggest challenge. His wife was always better at that, filling in his mind when absentmindedness got the better of him—kicking him under the table for a social slur or gently pointing to a missed button.

By early evening, we all welcomed a quiet darkness. "Could we watch a movie?" my father asked my husband and me. "We could all watch it on our big bed," he said with the hopefulness of a child searching for soft comfort. He wanted a buttery bowl of popcorn, just like his wife used to make.

I wish I could say that when we hugged him goodbye the following morning, I knew he would be just fine, surrounded by family and friends. But the truth is, I'm not sure. We did call him when we landed and he assured us he was fine—about to go to his Pilates class. The best I can do at this point, is what I try and do with my own children. And that is to believe in them during their struggles—which is truly the most powerful gift we can receive.

Published in the
Denver Post, January 2008

In Celebration of Colonoscopies

Age fifty can be wonderful, challenging and a major turning point in our lives. It's also the year of the colonoscopy. Statistics show colon cancer is the second leading cause of death in the United States, but as more people sign up for routine colonoscopies the number of deaths has begun decreasing.

When I heard from an old friend that her husband was diagnosed with stage four-colon cancer, I finally dialed the clinic number—a phone number I'd carried on a small piece of paper buried inside my appointment book for over a year. I was so frightened by the "prep" one would think I was scheduling major surgery, where full recovery would take anywhere from six to twelve months. The colonoscopy preparation and procedure actually take only twenty-four hours—far from an extended hospital stay followed by visiting nurses.

My appointment was three weeks away, far enough to write it in my calendar, and ignore the date for eighteen days. On day nineteen I stocked up on enough yogurt, chicken broth and ginger ale for a small community to have colonoscopies.

I kept my schedule open in the morning. So as my kids rushed out the door for school, eating leftover

Chinese food, I stood at the sink drinking glasses of a cherry flavored medicine (3 liters total), that bordered on unpleasant—closer to horrible. When I explained the procedure to my daughter, she appropriately answered, "Gross." I told myself the sooner I finished the present glass, the sooner I could fold laundry, lie down, or vacuum—all of which were better than drinking the colon prep liquid.

I'm don't usually wear a bathrobe and socks at 10:00 a.m. on a weekday morning. Even our golden retriever seemed to be asking, "What's up? Are we going to daycare or not?" When the phone rang, I was curious who'd be calling. A friendly young woman named Carolyn, introduced herself as a wine representative, asking if I was interested in broadening my palate. My palate was in need of something, but I didn't think Carolyn could help. I politely answered, "We really aren't big wine people," and hung up. I didn't know wine representatives called people.

When I arrived for my procedure with my very clean colon, I felt strangely relieved. It was the same way I felt taking my licensing exam: preparing for it was the worst part. But this time I could peacefully sleep, which isn't exactly the case with licensure. A smiling nurse wished me goodnight and I awakened to find my husband holding my hand. I left the building with photos of my terminal ileum and colon—all appearing normal. In my younger years, those ultrasound photos were always reassuring, because they were a celebration of my children growing within. And now at 51, it still remains a celebration, offering continued hope for many years of health and well-being. And the truth is, the reality of cancer is much more frightening than three liters of cherry fluid.

A Cookie Swap with Polish

The soft pink of my nail polish matches the gentleness of the Vietnamese women at my nail shop. A few years ago I decided I wanted nicer hands and was drawn to the lighted sign outside a nail salon: Walk-Ins Welcome.

"Can we help you today?" chimed a small Asian woman watching the weather channel on an overhead television set.

"Just a manicure," I answered shyly.

"Oh, you want acrylics," she encouraged, looking at my hands.

I nodded like an adolescent going along with the crowd. She guided me to a small table covered with tiny bottles my daughter would love. When she placed her white mask on, my anxiety grew. I tried to keep my priorities in order—anything for nice nails. She applied heady-smelling glue, followed by the acrylic. Then the drill for filing—loud and sending pieces of plastic into the air. We hadn't gotten to the polish, and already I felt exhausted.

"Best to get your keys and pay me first before polish," she instructed. Soon I sat at the drying table, holding my hands just so to avoid the slightest smudge. Because I was an amateur, I tried to reach for my car keys too early. She patiently guided me back to her table and re-applied light pink to my thumbs. I was afraid she wanted to change the sign to: *Walk-Ins Welcome, Experience Preferred*.

I left the shop both thanking her, apologizing and staring at my new hands. I now return every few weeks, opting for a simple manicure. I soon declined the fake nails, preferring to feel the softness of my husband's skin during lovemaking.

My relationship with Van and her family has grown closer over the years. We share stories and secrets and like to laugh. I bring fresh baked cookies and coffeecake; they massage my hands with soft cream. One snowy Friday afternoon I mentioned to Van that I was entering the annual baking contest to raise money for charity. "Oh, I'd like to learn to make cookies like you," she commented, as she instructed me to wash my hands before the polish.

This would be a challenging recipe exchange across cultures. Vietnamese has no comparable words to English teaspoons and tablespoons. Vanilla and chocolate chips didn't exist in Van's kitchen cupboard, nor did she have white flour or sugar. I tried to explain about cookie sheets—flat pans with no sides. Fractions are difficult in a new language. I thought we could go together to the baking aisle in Safeway, since the shop wasn't too busy. But our plans changed when three gum chewing teenagers arrived asking for "just a fill" and French manicures.

I was always surprised by the hours Van and her family kept in the shop. When I mentioned their hard work, she said, "Oh, no. This easy. The fields in Vietnam hard and no money."

As I left that day, I wondered about the juxtaposition of chocolate chip cookies and the fields of Vietnam. I remembered the cookie baking class I organized for friends a year earlier. Everyone arrived with a bowl, spoon and chocolate chips. Eight women around our kitchen table provided the most important ingredient: laughter. Batches of cookies were taken from the oven, all a little different, matching our individuality. Show and pretense were left out as we focused on good dough consistency. Next time, I'd invite Van.

The following morning, in preparation for the baking contest, I searched through my straw basket of recipes. The old magazine and newspaper cutouts were as sweet as the cookies themselves. Buried in-between Mrs. Step's lemon bread and Mom's oatmeal cookies, I found the chocolate pecan cookie recipe. I'd invented it for Passover, where cups of ground pecans became the sweet flour. I sorted through our cluttered, clangy utensil drawer, finding extra teaspoons and measuring cups. As I baked, I put aside a baking care package for Van—cups, spoons, brown sugar, baking soda and chocolate chips. My thoughts were mixed along with the pecans and sugar. I wanted to create a winning entry and also figure out a way to teach Van how to pull plump cookies from her own oven.

I emptied Valentine chocolates from a red box on our counter. Lining it with pink tissue paper, I gently placed my baked cookies inside. When I arrived to drop off my entry, I was greeted by chocolate masterpieces—Harry Potter characters, chocolate violins, and a leaning cake tower of Pisa. I smiled tentatively as I handed over my small pink box of cookies, a little like leaving one of my children at daycare. I left quickly; reassuring myself it was all for a good cause, blue ribbons weren't important.

I stopped in at the nail shop on my way home, excited to share my baking care package. I'd slipped an index card inside, detailing my recipe, along with a small secret: Always mix the dough with your hands. Van hugged me, surrounded by woman sitting peacefully, fingers outstretched, touching a culture I have come to love.

Published in the
Christian Science Monitor, December 2007

77 Birthday Cakes

As a wife and mother, I've baked 77 birthday cakes. That includes the cakes I carefully packaged for my sons after they went away to college. The cake was often chocolate chip banana bread, because butter-cream icing doesn't travel well in a shoebox. I started my cake baking career with small cupcakes, graduating to Barbie cakes, Batman cakes, train cakes, fire engines, bicycles, cars, castles, caterpillars, roller coasters, rainbows, hearts, and giant chocolate chip cookies. Over the years I've discovered luscious white, chocolate, and poppy seed cake recipes—the recipes themselves having butter and sugar smudges of years gone by. When our puppy was young, my recipes mysteriously disappeared off the counter before I realized she was chewing my cherished index cards like a tasty treat.

A new mom recently asked me, "Were you ever sad on your children's birthdays?" I came to understand my cakes were my way to grieve and celebrate in one sweet creation.

I remember whipping up pink icing for my daughter's Barbie cake, red icing for the fire engine, and black butter cream for Batman. The colors and sweetness represented a mother's tender feelings of joy and sadness. Like a sculptress, I'd carefully cut and shape moist cakes, making tiny monuments and paying tribute to how far we'd all come as I nurtured our family through the growing up years. My husband always clicked a picture of the cake sitting regally on the counter as though having a life of its own. Each cake had a number in the line of cakes before it, proud to be part of such a celebratory and exclusive club.

As my children eagerly talked about their parties, friends, and gift wishes, I always asked the all-important question: "What are you thinking about for the cake?" There was always that age—the crossover point, like with Santa, when excitement about the cake lost some of its luster. "I don't know Mom, it doesn't really matter." I tried to hide my disappointment, reassuring myself that growing up was what they were supposed to do. Did I really expect my 16-year-old to jump with excitement about his chocolate car cake, given the sweetest gift was his driving license?

A small, old fashioned cake supply store in our town is owned by a soft-spoken gray haired lady who always recognized me a few times a year. "And what shape are you baking this time?" She'd ask. She helped me pick out the right size white cardboard and doily with the same care as someone seeking the perfect dress for a special occasion. Birthday candles lined one wall—tiny lipstick candles, pencil candles, baseball and football candles, little guitars and musical notes, tiny telephones and tulips. She'd ring my purchases up slowly—adding them on a small note pad and punching the amount into a register that seemed as old as her thin and bumpy wrinkled hands. I always worried that one day I'd pull up to find the store closed because the time had come for her to have no more birthdays. But it still stands as a tribute to no one ever being too old for birthday cakes.

My husband always asks for a healthy version—something with soymilk and wheat flour. And so I experiment with soy butter and organic sugars like a traveler learning a foreign language. And somehow, since love is the same across cultures, the message remains universal even without pink icing.

I recently learned the Vietnamese only celebrate a child's first birthday. And each year after, on the Chinese New Year, everyone celebrates their birthdays together for the coming year. Which is the message nestled between the layers of all my cakes. Each birthday is a passage for everyone. The cake has become my gift to all of us, as we taste a small slice of yesterday and tomorrow, celebrating the life of one family.

A Sweet Summer Fling

I never did get to say good-bye to Wilma. We had a summer relationship when I bought sacks of her juicy Colorado peaches. Always in mid-July on a warm Saturday morning, we'd meet at the farmer's market. Her wooden table was decorated with full crates of yellow/orange peaches—small white sacks brimming with soft, delicate fruit. Her old red delivery truck announced her arrival, the Santa of all peaches. Even when I arrived behind many other customers, her smiling eyes over the tops of their heads made me feel special. She wore a cozy denim shirt covered by a peach stained apron. She'd wipe her hands clean—creases in her palms holding quiet secrets of her working life. Like my home baked chocolate chip cookies, Wilma's peaches were always good, and often delicious.

A German farmwoman from the western slope of Colorado, I imagined she led the life I'd read about in books where writers described their childhood on the farm harvesting fruit, gathering family love in bushels that made no one want to grow up. We always found time to talk, catching up on the past fall and winter we'd been apart.

"I've been well," I say. "I did have a sad miscarriage in January, but I'm healing."

"Oh, honey, I'm so sorry. You go slow now." She comforted me like a grandmother.

Wilma didn't tell me much about her life, so I was left to imagine apple picking and pressing cider, followed by a peacefully cold white winter. She liked to put a bag together for me, picking out the plumpest peaches she could find and then topping the sack off with tiny pears—like sprinkles on an ice-cream cone. I never paid full price and would always return the following week with peach muffins or soft slices of peach coffeecake to complete our unspoken deal. One summer I finally made the connection that all the grocery stores sold the same western slope peaches. But hers tasted better, her sacking my peaches was part of it. Organic peaches were sold down the way, next to the goat cheese people. Many people passed Wilma in order to buy organically. At the time I didn't realize how important the organic issue would be to our relationship.

As our summer Saturdays became Saturdays in September, I had to prepare myself for our goodbye. I wanted to be sure of the last day so I wouldn't be caught off guard. We'd make plans that next summer, I'd make the six hour drive with my family to visit her farm—perhaps around the annual peach festival. The last day I always bought a crate of peaches to make them last as long as possible. She taught me how to boil them up so the skin would just slide off; then slice and sprinkle them with a special powder to keep their color when I'd freeze them. Into October I could eat peaches, putting off having to completely let go.

I didn't know the letting go would have to be final until last Saturday morning at the luscious start of peach season. Wilma was gone. I asked the lettuce, tomato, and cucumber vender if he knew anything about Wilma.

"Oh, they didn't ask her back. She wasn't organic enough."

My peaches suddenly felt contaminated without Wilma. You can't get more down to earth than how Wilma cultivated and sold those peaches. I guess no one really understood the richness of the soil of our summer relationship.

Published in the
Washington Post, August 2006

There's a Man in My Kitchen

It's an early morning in August; just two more weekends before my son leaves for college. His college list reads: refrigerator, shower sandals, extra long sheets, plastic soap dish, laptop—at least 17 in. screen, no firearms. Before he was born our list was pampers, crib bumpers and blunt nail scissors.

He knows not to wash whites and darks together, not to eat fries every day, drink enough water, drive slow and sober and don't be late for class, job, or the dentist. He doesn't know what it will be like not to bump into me in the kitchen, beat his brother in ping-pong, let the puppy out, and remind me to buy more ketchup. The blare of his car stereo will no longer rock me awake and the sounds of Fantasy Football will be absent every Sunday.

I watch him by the kitchen counter, slicing a small piece of avocado, a dollop of goat cheese atop a sesame seed cracker, when it only used to be Big Macs. He chews and leans just like my husband. They both have long legs, wear khaki shorts just above the knee. My son's shorts now fit him; his boxers kept neatly out of sight. He works at a clothing store and finds good deals for his younger brother, talks to his 11 year old sister like a normal person, drops her at friends' houses, and asks me how I felt after my latest 10K race. Who is this nice man in my kitchen? Yesterday he wasn't here.

I hadn't even finished reading the paper the morning the middle school principal called. "Hello, Ned Simons here. I have your son, Ben, in my office..." I drove recklessly out to school to discuss the pros and cons of cigarette smoking before first period. We stopped at the grocery store on the way home and all I wanted to do was stick him back in the cart, his pudgy hands holding tight, smiling at Cheerios I chose off the shelf. Instead I screamed about cancer and ranted about trust issues. My son sullenly asked for pepperoni Hotpockets. Not too long after he turned 16 and we were at a police auction bidding eighty dollars for his first car, a rusty white Toyota with two broken headlights. Then he got his first job sacking groceries, his first girlfriend with straight blond hair, ACTs, SATs, and two speeding tickets. Suddenly he was handing me his high school diploma in a blue padded folder.

He tentatively says, "Mom, no offense, but I think I want only Dad to take me to school." My friends tell me it's normal not to want your Mommy at college, especially if she does that crying thing. What he doesn't know is that his father will also do the crying thing. When he lost his umbilical cord, I remember joking about the next step being college. His bedroom is loosing its messy luster and new socks and boxers lie next to folded t-shirts, shorts and oversized tennis sneakers without blinking lights in the heels.

His plane leaves in two weeks, the first day my daughter starts middle school and my other son enters tenth grade. For so long I have worked to be an attentive, involved mother and now this Jewish mother must learn to let go. I am an emotional surveyor, always trying to measure accurate distance from my children, each one needing different distances at different times. The college distance is new, making me want to stand on my tiptoes and kiss the cheek of this gentle man in my kitchen who leans down with a smile that says, "Goodbye, Mom."

Published in the
Washington Post, September 2005

Recollections of the Bike Centennial - Pedaling Across the Divide

It's a hot summer night and I won't sit until I find my old blue photo album and the small journal that goes with it. Our closets brim with dusty boxes in piles that have been on a tilt for decades—frozen in time. They only get wobbly as I start rummaging, disrupting an order that has been at peace for years. My 19-year-old son's return home for the summer has dusted off my memory. Thirty years ago at age 19, I pedaled from Virginia to Oregon on a white Peugeot 10 speed. My son is peddling wares at a clothing store; I chose to pedal 4200 miles across the country.

My son and I have in common cresting the hill into our 20's; I chose to literally sweat my way toward increased independence. My mother fretted for 80 days straight the summer of 1976. She only allowed me to go if I put a postcard in the mail every day and remembered to eat enough. Like with my younger kids who have to call when they change locations, my postcards documented every small town from Lightfoot, Virginia to Reedsport, Oregon. My father diligently charted my course on state road maps, a red marker outlining the journey.

A bike route crosses the United States on back roads designed to teach you history as you pedal.

Organized by Bike-Centennial and established in 1976, two thousand cyclists crossed the country in either direction. My group of sixteen met for the first time one hot sticky morning at a Virginia campground. We ranged in age from sixteen to sixty, coming from as many states as we were about to visit. We were big, small, in shape and not in shape. Lois, a 50-year-old woman, (I viewed her as old) packed up after two days. It wasn't quite the "interesting" summer she'd expected. We traveled roughly 60 miles a day, carrying a sleeping bag and panniers of light clothing. We always had a roof over our heads in churches, elementary schools, or foreign legion halls.

As promised, I ate my three meals a day, breakfast and dinner at old time cafes with pies under glass covers decorating the counter. Sixty miles a day wasn't too much given we had an easy 12 hours to get from old town point A to old town point B. We rose early, learning our individual routines as the days passed along with the states. We'd cycle in twos and threes, matching personality and pedaling speed. I chose 26-year-old Robyn, blond and freckled, studying to be a horse vet. And then 16-year-old Scott from Alabama, who we adopted. His gangly awkwardness left him out of the small cool crowd of two other sixteen-year-old boys from Scarsdale.

The three of us watched out for each other. Often we were victims of both weather and terrain. The Virginia Ozarks and Kentucky Appalachians greeted us early on. The roads weren't switchbacks, but often just straight up. Coal trucks chugged up, coming dangerously close, treating us like annoying flies. Our small swarm protected us from just being swatted. A day at a time helped in the beginning: just biking to the evening meal, which was often grilled cheese and sweet fruit pies with a delicious Crisco crust before anyone knew we shouldn't eat such things.

Kansas blew in after Missouri. My son described a Bar Mitzvah as, "just when you think it's over, it goes on for another two hours." Kansas was like that. The headwinds pushed against us as we inched from one corn field to the next. I both loved and hated the challenge. But somehow the simplicity of sun and sweat was actually a cool breeze in the midst of becoming a grown-up. For ten weeks, I could just go on a bike ride. And since we were passing through towns named Pippa Passes, Troutville, Boonesville, Elkorn City, Falls of Rough, and Eddyville, I could cherish time standing still.

Windy Kansas flatlands soon rolled into Colorado mountains and a blue water sky that kept me looking up. My New York childhood sky was lower and heavier. I breathed differently out west. I had more air at higher altitude. The Rocky Mountain roads were switchbacks, encouraging our ascent instead of making us second guess our two wheeling journey. We were empowered as we flew down mountain passes smiling recklessly, with no helmets—except for bearded Bob who donned his helmet every morning, with a tiny rear view mirror attached.

Cyclists traveling west to east would alert us about life ahead and we'd do the same for them— where to find hot showers, watch for the cookie lady passing out snickerdoodles, and take a left to swim in a clear lake. Every 10 days we had a rest day where we bought little boxes of detergent to wash our gym shorts and t-shirts so they could feel brand new. We took naps and went bowling.

Wyoming, Montana and Idaho escorted us into Oregon where we started pedaling more slowly.

Unspoken ambivalence took the air from our tires. Our last day of pedaling went late into the night. We stopped in a Redwood forest, lounging against our bikes, using them like pillows—their comfort and security had taken us so far. The Pacific Ocean no longer beckoned us. We told each other bedtime stories created from our free wheeling journey. It was a mourning before dawn. A dawn that held only a hint of my grown-up life out west—where I'd marry and we'd raise our three children under a big western sky.

Thirty years have passed since that starry summer. And now I watch my son slowly pedaling away, balancing the best he can as his back tire is nestled in childhood, his front tire spinning into tomorrow.

Condensed version published in
Bicycling Magazine, April 2007

Where U-Turns Are Legal

A two day visit to Florida felt like going around the world and back. It was Parents Weekend at my son's college and at the last minute, the mother "pull" said to go, no matter cost or distance from Boulder.

My son often says, "It's just so different out here—people and place." In simple terms, the streets are lined with palm trees and malls. He spends time on jet skis instead of a snowboard. People only drink hot coffee in the morning. You have to carry a sweater for the air-conditioning, and your compass becomes the beach instead of the mountains.

South Florida isn't one culture, but many woven together into an intricate tapestry. A friendly Romanian woman showed my daughter the best color eye shadow for her skin tone. A Brazilian waiter served us pancakes and the Haitian hotel clerk helped me log onto the Internet. Woven into the beauty of these cultures are the large churches and synagogues alongside the marvel of Jewish delis with herring, noodle kuegel and tubs of lox cream cheese filling their display cases. Shopping malls the size of airports, have their own culture sporting Juicy Couture, Tiffany's and Coach with gorgeous women who wear it all.

Nestled inside is the college culture. My son lives in an off-campus apartment with a Guinness poster and Broncos banner above his couch. His freezer is stocked with pizza, waffles and chicken breasts. "I'm learning to sauté chicken with olive oil and lots of garlic," he comments proudly. This is another new world for me—my son's kitchen, where he buys his own cereal and Gatorade and asks if he can get me anything for lunch. His cell phone rings often and he answers with, "I'll call you later—with family now."

"What is it for you that's so different out here?" I ask.

He pauses, thinks a moment, rubbing his palm against his jeans. "It's like the girl in my English class who arrives every day, all dressed, make-up, fancy sunglasses she uses to check her reflection, then fiddles with not one cell-phone but two which she pulls from her Prada bag."

I glanced down at my Teva sandals and realized my son, born to psychologist parents in Colorado, is trying to make sense of this Florida tapestry from a different angle, searching for the pattern in these varied values. He takes my plate and begins to wash it at the sink. "Sometimes I think I feel more certain about me than my friends do, but sometimes maybe not."

My eyes watered when I said goodbye to this man with sparkling eyes like his father's. My trip was quick and I didn't spend much time on campus, but I learned what I needed to know. In south Florida, U-turns are legal, which is reassuring to all of us from different places trying to find our way. And as my son finds his own direction, what better place than streets lined with Palm trees, fertilized by soil from around the world?

Published in
The Miami Herald, November 2006

Emancipating Layla

We never considered puppy daycare until Layla, our golden retriever puppy, ate my husband's I-Pod. Since my husband and I grew up with wild golden retrievers, we had worked hard not to repeat our childhood dog dysfunction. Layla proudly graduated from puppy class after eight weeks where we'd joined twelve owners, their dogs, and one teacher who obviously had a perfect dog at home. He carried a clicker, and shouted above the yipping dogs and confused, exhausted owners. "Keep your pups close. Reward 1-2-3, pet, reward. Good, now repeat: 1-2-3, reward. Good! Now wait, reward, spin, 1-2-3!" Layla and I danced through the class feeling proud of our accomplishments. However we never covered the issue of keeping one's dog away from I-Pods.

In defense of Layla's parenting, we aren't stay at home owners, but we lovingly run Layla every morning and evening and do ball throwing in between. On snowy mornings, Layla is like a toddler in snowsuit and mittens celebrating snow for the first time. She gleefully approaches other runners always, assuming they're as happy to see her, as she is to see them. Throwing the ball at dusk can be meditative as a pale orange setting sun frames her bounding body—

skillfully catching a worn tennis ball in mid-air. Chewed shoes and socks, and even dollar bills eaten off the counter—we've taken those in stride, but the I-pod incident became the defining moment. Layla needed more quality time with other dogs, and we just aren't dogs.

What surprised me most was my reaction. My husband encouraged checking out Doggie Depot just a few blocks away. But I worried Layla might experience it as abandonment—whereas good owners have dogs who peacefully lie in their beds during the day, never causing a stir. My three children are way beyond daycare, but my feelings were similar. No matter how warm and loving their daycare home felt, the hand off held a mother's ambivalence. I've always loved dogs, but was never confused by who was the dog and who were the children—until perhaps this week.

We certainly never had puppy daycare as kids, but we also had no leashes. Children seem to have gained more freedom over the years, as dogs have lost some. Supervised separations from owners are inevitable. Running free around the neighborhood is something from the olden days, along with biking without a helmet, Clark candy bars, and the "Wizard of Oz" televised once a year.

So in the same week, we planned a Seattle college visit with my high school son, and Layla began puppy daycare three mornings a week. She has her own hook for her leash. She arrives in time for warm-ups and welcome, followed by free play and an hour of structured Frisbee and ball throwing. We pick her up after snack and naptime. So far we have not been asked to attend parent/teacher conferences.

She's panting, happy and exhausted when she arrives home, and I'm left with wondering why Doggie

Depot unleashed so many feelings. The truth is, all of life's separations bring up leavings in general. Layla brought me the gift of facing some of the more human transitions of the past year. Turning fifty and downsizing our lives into a smaller home as my middle son walks out the front door toward college feels like opening a fortune cookie that reads, "Big changes, hold onto your hat!"

But in truth, the sadness of our farewells is the tender watering for growth. So as I watch Layla's beautiful energy on a snowy field, I'm reminded that the glory of separation is also the celebration of freedom. Leavings allow our children to find themselves, giving us the chance to unwrap unopened gifts. Separation is a blessing to find our version of that simple yellow tennis ball. And may we all bound into the next stage of our lives with the gusto of a golden retriever who confidently assumes she will be loved by everyone.

Dog Paddling Pups

On a gorgeous, blue sky Sunday, we grab towels and sunscreen and pack the car for the Scott Carpenter Pool. But we aren't going swimming. This is all for Layla our loveable golden retriever puppy, because the Labor Day closing of the neighborhood pool is all day dog swim.

Many summer days when our three children were young, my husband and I would pile them into the car for heat and stress relief at the pool. But now they're with friends, enjoying the last days of summer, free from swim bubbles we'd strap on them for safety. And my husband and I are left doting over Layla. As we back out of the driveway, my husband smiles at our neighbors who are herding their frolicking pup into their van. Bailey is Layla's sister and she's also going for a swim, as their children are off socializing without swim bubbles.

We drive into the parking lot, slowly finding a parking space, careful not to bump into any eager dogs or smiling owners. Layla bolts out of the car doing her "wiggle" dance. Everyone is nice as she greets them, her leash trailing behind, my husband patiently trying to grab hold. The pool is a dog's heaven—a dog park with a swimming pool. I had the great idea to bring the Sunday NY Times; no one would drown as I dreamed about traveling to the exotic places written about in the Travel section. My dream soon became soggy as Layla enjoyed jumping in, and then bounding over to shake herself dry while standing on the Arts and Leisure section.

I watched her run around the pool, go close to the edge, back away and then wade slowly in to the shallow end, nabbing her tennis ball. It felt like watching my kids on the soccer field. They were active, good runners but tentative. They weren't soccer stars like the neighbor children; they were just out there having fun. Layla kept up the family name; her sister was jumping and diving like a seal, while Layla was tentatively having the time of her life.

My husband encouraged her the best he could without stripping down and joining the swimmers. He'd lovingly pet her, then encourage her to focus on the fuzzy tennis ball as he threw it across the pool and shouted, "Go get it, Layla!" After about 45 minutes Layla was showing promise, retrieving the ball, but getting out as soon as possible.

As I watched the two of them, I remembered that when our previous dog died, my husband said, "No more dogs, this is too hard!" I was in no rush either, until the day I held soft, tiny Layla. But my husband took some convincing. I don't think he ever agreed to get Layla; he was just outnumbered four to one. As I watched his commitment to teaching her to swim, and then saw him dry her with not one big towel but two, I knew he'd fallen in love again. As for Layla, she was asleep in the backseat by the time we'd left the parking lot.

Published in the
Boulder Camera, September 2006

And the Envelope Please

My son, a senior in high school, is in the middle of the college application process. When he received his first response in the mail from one of his choices, both my husband and I stared nervously at the envelope on the counter.

"Do you think it's thick or thin?" I asked.

"Definitely on the thicker side," my husband assured me.

So much is different now than in the days when I applied. But the hope for the thick versus thin envelope remains timeless.

Sometime last summer, although my son seemed quite calm about impending applications, I started to feel a little overwhelmed. How does a good parent support a child through a process with so much emotion weaved in to the importance of grades, test scores, deadlines, finances, geography, size, weather and interests?

I remember filling out just one college application, to a small, cold school in upstate New York, that I later transferred from. So I was no expert in this area. We decided that a few meetings with a college adviser might free my son from a parent's anxiety.

And now that he has successfully completed essays and SATs, and envelopes are sealed, I relax a bit, but still hold on to a mother's worry.

My first two years of college had some good times, mostly dear friendships holding us all together as we tried to grow up avoiding disaster. Weekends were spent studying, with nights at fraternity parties, our feet sticking to spilled beer all together as we tried to grow up avoiding disaster.

I coped with the stress by running two times a day, skirting snowdrifts and eating a lot of runny cafeteria cottage cheese. The scale was my iron mother, providing comfort and security for every pound I lost.

And then, at the end of my sophomore year, I telephoned home in tears. "Dad, I have to get out of here; this isn't the place for me."

Within a few months, I was on a plane to Boulder and unpacking my life at the University of Colorado. And now, 30 years later, I am the mom, hoping my son will have a smoother ride.

Recently we visited two colleges in the Pacific Northwest. Bundled in hats and mittens, we toured campuses and were always relieved to find shelter in academic buildings. When I asked my son how he thought he'd do with the weather, he answered, "You know beautiful weather isn't that important to me."

This is what feels so different than in years past. Kids are asked, "What do you want?" versus the primary focus on a good school wanting them. My son brought questions that he wanted to ask his college interviewer. I remember only worrying about the impression I'd make on the interviewer, with less concern for my needs or my impressions of the college. I believe that the goal needs to be the search for the right match versus the "right" school.

The weekend brought my son more clarity about

where he hoped to attend college. It brought us the opportunity to spend a whole weekend with our son, which felt like a rare pearl.

I smiled remembering his innocent question as a toddler.

"Is it possible for a son to be smarter than his mommy and daddy?"

My answer has always been the same, "Yes." And I continue to believe so much wiser.

Published in the Denver Post, February 2008

Farewell to Two Men

This summer, I'm saying goodbye to two men in my family. My son is leaving for college and my father is losing his mind. My stepmother called to tell me my father had fallen and was on his knees in his hospital room—he'd forgotten he couldn't walk. My son contemplates his first college semester, walking out on his own. And I stand between them, trying to find my footing.

I used to organize the come and go of toddler play dates. I now plan for my son's return flight home at Christmas. I print his itinerary with sadness between the lines. And I have to remind myself that our kids do return—first from the neighbor's and then from across the country. But a father's mind doesn't return; for Dementia is a one-way ticket.

Although I've already done the college thing once before with my older son, saying goodbye never feels easy or the same. All three of my children are so different. It is said, no sibling has the same parents: thus no parents have the same children. So as I say goodbye to my dark-haired son, having already sent his older fair-haired brother off, it all feels new—except for my watery eyes.

When my son hit ninth grade, suddenly I became really irritating, and by tenth grade I was intolerable.

In those years, if one more mother told me what a great kid he was, I thought I'd hit her. But as he walks out our front door, he's become a truly lovely man. We talk to each other now. I've learned to ask fewer questions, listen, and never do the therapist thing of introducing the four-letter word *feel* into any conversation. At 18 he's become low maintenance, and as long as there's enough Arizona iced tea, bagels, turkey, ham and potato chips, he doesn't seem to need me. I still steal up to his bedroom to gather dirty socks and t-shirts and stay long enough to throw his maroon comforter over soft sheets—like chocolate sprinkles on ice-cream, it's a mother's topping off.

In contrast, my Dad has become high maintenance. He was Papa Mike to my kids—a grandpa-like super hero who had root beer in the refrigerator, dollars in his pocket and a pool in which he taught them to dive. And since he was successful when he had his wits about him, he's fortunate to have a care-giving army to support him during his final battle. But even his army can't fight off the devastating effects of Dementia. How ironic that a weak and deteriorating mind is such a powerful force affecting my father and all of us who lovingly bid him farewell. And like saying goodbye to our children, the goodbye never feels easy or practiced, but both sad and timely.

My son is beginning to clean out his closet, tossing away old sneakers, school papers and too tight t-shirts. My father searches through darkened closets in his mind for lost memories. My son shows me a dusty middle school project, "My Grandfather's Success Story." Even though my father has forgotten his landmarks, his children and grandchildren have not.

But my tender tears remind me of the "good" in

good-bye. For my son, the ride will only get better, fueled by the love of generations before. For my father, I hope it is a gentle downhill to the finish. And for myself, I'm certain a mother's closet holds unfound treasures—once the children's beds have been made one last time.

Published in the
Denver Post, August 2008

Tears and Target

When my son lost his umbilical cord, I smiled and said to my husband, "The next step is college." And what seems like a day later, we've taken that next step as we return from Seattle where our son is beginning his freshman year. Under a beautiful northwestern sky, our tears became the only raindrops. My son allowed me to hug him tighter than I had in years as he gently bent down to rest his cheek on my shoulder.

I wish I could say the whole weekend was back-to-back tender moments, but as in the previous four years, he spent a lot of time dodging me as I tried my best to keep up with the forever two-step dance of parenting. "Mom, PLEASE stop bringing up the issue of something to hang on my walls!" and "Do you have to talk to everyone?"

Move-in day began with instructions for all Seward Hall third-floor students to arrive at 9:00 a.m. to reduce duffle/box/suitcase congestion on stairways. I made my first error when we were signing in next to a young woman who coincidently was from our hometown. I had the nerve to introduce myself, which invited a glare from my son that quickly let me know I was completely out of line. Thankfully, when we opened the door to room 316 and were greeted by his new roommate and parents, introductions became acceptable as my son shook his roommate's hand with a smile. As we all climbed over boxes, bedding, and guitar cases, we thought if we made the necessary Target trip right then it might make the unpacking easier for his roommate. In truth, I think we all yearned for the security of those red concentric circles.

Typically, a Target store materializes a few miles from most college campuses. We drove three blocks, took a right, and saw the familiar red circles that embraced a small family feeling a little lost. I clutched the list scribbled on the back of the rental car agreement as we grabbed two carts and began our journey. Similar trios or dyads surrounded us; the common denominator was a son or daughter for whom shopping with one or two parents was a necessary but irritating experience. I was reassured when I heard a son announce to his mother, "I really don't care what color the rug is! Just pick one!"

Piled high with hangers, a bulletin board, rolls of two sided tape, detergent, a peanut butter jar, pens, notebooks, mugs, cereal boxes, and a trash can, I happily checked things off—feeling in control of something. Animal crackers sat invitingly at the check-out counter, but somehow wouldn't match my son's shaving crème and small Guinness poster.

After we hauled everything up three flights of stairs that felt like six, my son brought up lunch.... for my husband and me. "I've got it covered here," he said bending over computer wires. Relieved, we found the nearest coffee shop and exhaled. We were exhausted and it was only noon. In truth, Target and stairways were the least of it. It had been a long eighteen years, and simultaneously wanting to leave as quickly as possible and stay together forever is an exhausting dilemma.

The day continued with parent workshops and wrapped up with convocation, a word that seems to be used only on college campuses. As we sat elbow to elbow on stadium bleachers I focused more on the families around us than on the college president's insights. The red-haired young woman next to me leaned in to her father and whispered, "I love you, Dad." My son, wearing his backwards baseball cap, was definitely not thinking how much he loved my husband and me. And in truth, at that moment, I wasn't thinking how much I loved him. I was thinking about dinner and wondering if I'd be sad or relieved when we said goodbye, and if we'd gotten everything on the list.

The following morning the "moment" in the parking lot arrived. I wanted to stop time for a minute, just to figure out how to do and say the right Mom thing. My son turned to me and as we looked each other in the eye, holding one another's gaze. Neither of us had to figure out anything. Our tears actually felt like a beautiful "Hello." I'd never felt the truth so poignantly as I did that morning. Saying goodbye to our children allows them to hold on tighter. It is a wonderful reminder that the umbilical chord will always remain an ever-changing golden thread between us.

Published in the
Denver/Boulder Women's Magazine, November 2008

One Child Left Behind - To Become a Woman

As we all try to stay educated about the latest turns in the economy and the election, lessons learned from our children remain timeless.

I opened the heavy front door into the high school hallway and my thirtieth "back to school night." The smell was old and dusty, yet alive with parents and the lasting whiff of students gone home for the day. I hold my daughter's schedule close, trying to read the room number of her Spanish class. I risk asking another wandering mother if she knows where room 242 might be. She smiles and answers, "I'm so sorry but I'm also lost," as she walks off, craning her neck to read the numbers on each door. We all have our heads bent back, looking upward, like lost, searching birds. "Are you my room number? Are you my room number?"

Although each teacher passes out a class syllabus, I'm not there to learn which Spanish words they will conjugate or when the next geography test is. Like most of my daughter's life, she doesn't include or believe she needs me much, until she wants a haircut appointment, money for lunch, or to have me proofread an English paper. I attend back to school night for the same reason I still make my children's beds. I find comfort in being where they have been, since being beside them isn't always welcomed. I follow in their footsteps from a comfortable distance, without intruding.

But the truth is, these high school halls filled with parents instead of students aren't the same halls that my daughter walks every day. As my daughter enters her freshman year, it isn't the stress of academics that she and her friends discuss behind closed doors. The apprehension before registration seemed more related to how well their pictures would come out on their i.d. cards. Given she's my youngest, I do know they grow up and their priorities will blossom beyond bosoms and beauty. We all had a dose of this international phenomenon where cultures teach values we mothers wish our young daughters would not be influenced by. The Chinese Olympic Committee decided a seven-year-old singer wasn't cute enough on stage, and replaced her with a prettier child to lip sync the words. Unfortunately they were unaware how unattractive their cruel gesture was and how ugly such superficiality can appear.

So, as a society, how can we raise our daughters to celebrate their bodies without being consumed by them? How can they accept the beauty of their cleavage without it being their main focus? And how can we stress the importance of the function of our bodies versus form?

On a recent shopping expedition, we found ourselves in the women's lingerie department. The saleswoman was pointing out the versatility of cleavage adjusters—bras that can be adjusted according to the occasion. For example, one can reduce cleavage at school and then enhance cleavage at a party, by one click of a clasp. Suddenly I feel thrown into a whole new world, given my daughter is blessed with bosoms while her mother was graced with a quieter body.

The challenge we face in parenting also extends to how we raise our sons. Cleavage is a two way street, and it's important to stress the importance of not objectifying women, with the hope that young men will eventually understand there's more to life than sex and sports. Lecturing our children is one way, but modeling is the most powerful teacher.

So as mothers and fathers it's up to us to embrace our bodies and sexuality with respect. I'm glad my daughter is developing breasts when I was developing an eating disorder. But even if our history doesn't include the pain of an eating disorder, most of us have a complicated relationship with our bodies and our sexuality. Our assignment as parents is to continue developing a healthy relationship with ourselves—homework that's a lifelong journey. As we proofread English papers and test our kids on vocabulary, we can't forget our requirements as parents. We can't leave ourselves behind as we encourage our children forward. For that is how we truly stay side by side—even as they walk without us in school hallways—learning to love and respect themselves and their bodies.

Published in the
Denver Post, November 2008

A Burning Lesson

For a clinical psychologist there's a steadfast rule: never answer a cell phone during a psychotherapy session. And last evening was no different. Except my phone continued to alert me with an annoying beep I would promptly silence until my kind patient said, "You know, I think someone needs you. Really, it's fine to take it." Reluctantly I agreed.

"This is Priscilla."

"Hi, this is Doggie Depot. Since you're being evacuated, we'd be happy to board Layla overnight."

That's how I learned of the North Boulder wildfire burning dangerously close to our home and many others. Suddenly I was caught in the "cross-fire" of my world and my patient's. Thankfully our meeting was finishing and her compassion made the awkward transition from her private world to my own a little smoother.

My husband and fifteen-year-old daughter picked me up on a dark, windy night—our car packed with what they each thought were the important belongings to grab, believing our home along with many others could be swept up in fast moving flames. My daughter appropriately packed up her closet, clothes sticking out of un-zipped suitcases, shoes and boots thrown in the trunk.

"Mom, I got your running shoes, computer, and a bunch of sweaters and a pair of jeans."

My husband handed me my reading glasses and the novel by my bed. I was comforted by how well they knew me. The three of us banded together, challenged more by our fears than any impending danger. We found security at our traditional Wednesday night restaurant. We planned our next step over burgers and baked potatoes, hoping the flames were a passing inconvenience. Denial seasoned our meal as we tried to make the evening feel like just another Wednesday. Fueled by our denial, we decided to drive toward home. A strange beauty of a lighted hillside silenced us as we approached the police blockade.

I'm not proud of our next decision, but our wish for security kept pushing us toward home. Police couldn't block all the routes, and truthfully they had more important things to do then deal with a rebellious family not wanting to listen. Many kind friends had invited us for sleepovers, but we felt safest at home grappling for some normalcy. We monitored the flaming hillside from our bedroom window with TV newscasters in the background reporting on the devastation, evacuations and uncertainty. Our daughter slept as my husband and I were reassured by calming flames and reports of containment.

By morning, the hillside was dominated by black brush and smoke taking the place of the previous night's frightening glamour. I took my daughter to school and my husband to work, pretending everything was normal. I was home in time for my morning run up the mountain. It was early enough that no yellow tape blocked the trail. A few people were walking their dogs next to smoldering brush as I ran past. My familiar climb was surrounded by dark, ravished earth. Suddenly nothing seemed normal about any of this. It was eerie and frightening, even though this was probably the safest I'd been in the last twelve hours. In spite of our decision to return, we were fortunate our safety was protected by the skill of hundreds of firefighters. The black hills lying dangerously close to our neighborhood outlined how much my husband and I had taken for granted. Next time, we'll find security by trusting the better judgment of those who are trying to keep us safe. And I hope I can forgive the adolescent in me who continues to try and just grow up.

Published in the
Boulder Camera, January 2009

Our Dirty Laundry

    I would never read my children's Facebook profiles, emails, or diaries but I do read their laundry. Clues about their teenage lives are hidden between the wrinkles of jeans and t-shirts. Sometimes I'll notice sweet smell of perfume in my son's collar or the whiff of aftershave in my daughter's green hoody. The sound of a forgotten lighter taps the walls of the shaking dryer. My children tell me the truth sometimes, but the real story lies nestled in their buttonholes, cuffs, and collars. Laundry is the gateway to my children's lives until they go away to college. And when they return for a visit, I find comfort in throwing their wrinkled pile into the washer.

    Unfortunately, over Spring Break, I shrunk my son's dark blue wool sweater and now it fits me perfectly. It wasn't on purpose—I just didn't see it lost among his crumpled high school t-shirts. I didn't know he owned such a fancy sweater; it wasn't with him when he left for college. He mentioned he'd gotten some good deals at a second hand store, proud that he was dressing a little spiffier these days. It's part of his emancipation, finding himself along with a more polished appearance. I felt terrible—good mothers are supposed to encourage separation and not "shrink" a son's emotional growth. Perhaps even better mothers would have sons do their own laundry. But laundry is a weakness of mine, along with making my children's beds and breakfast. I did replace the sweater with one I found on sale, but I was surprised by how guilty I felt. The truth is, as I celebrate my kids walking out the front door, there is no back door to sadness. Somehow the shrinking sweater reminded me of a small part of me that quietly says, " Go, but...wait, don't go."

My son called home one Sunday in September asking, "Mom, what's the deal with the wrinkles when I pull my clothes out of the dryer?"

"Just make sure you don't overload it and they'll do better."

"Thanks! Gotta go."

Laundry is one of the ways we stay connected. His care packages often contain both chocolate chip cookies and a roll of quarters. When we helped him move in, we bought Tide at Target: it's the smell he knows.

When it comes to my husband, I find no surprises in his laundry and I'm quite sure he would find none in mine. Perhaps that's a reassuring sign of a good marriage. Our dirty laundry holds no secrets. And yet with our children, growing up means laundry filled with both wrinkles and mystery.

When I'm away my husband does the laundry. He neatly folds; building organized but mixed up piles. I find my daughter's shorts next to my running shorts and she finds my socks and t-shirts piled in with her jeans and underwear. I'm sure he finds no loss in not knowing what belongs to whom. But as a mother I cherish knowing my children's wardrobe. It's a way to take care without opening closet doors and intruding into their blossoming lives. So for now I will hold onto the traditional side of me and continue the daily cycle of laundry, feeling a closeness to my children who wave goodbye wearing a mother's embrace.

Running is My Passport

Whenever I travel east, I pack lightly for a short trip, since childhood baggage can sometimes be heavy. I always wear my running shoes, as they're hard to fit in my small backpack.

It is raining as I splatter through puddles in New York's Central Park on my early morning run. I'm avoiding the same puddles I saw a few months earlier on the day my stepmother died. Now I face a similar sadness as my father lies in ICU. Running is my passport; it tells me who I am during life's travels. Running on gray sidewalks feels so different than my rhythm on mountain trails back home. I skirt between open umbrellas instead of the brush of golden Aspen trees, searching for a forest freedom that New Yorkers only find on vacation.

Like racing, the pace of change in our family has gone quickly in the last few months. From a funeral to a wedding—after my step-mother died, my father at 86 fell in-love with smiley, silver haired Audrey and got married in a tuxedo only wearing one sock. "I was just so nervous," he confided after the ceremony. But now I see it was the beginning of his confusion that makes it hard for him to find speech instead of his other sock.

My father's doctor is a young woman who wears a

long cotton skirt and Nikes. She too must find solace on a morning run before traveling across the border to "hospital country" with cool temperatures and no sunlight where the natives are the sick people, the tourists—their family and friends. I lean close to my father, smelling the antiseptic of white hospital blankets replacing his aftershave. His speech is halting and garbled and when I catch a word I understand, it's like fireflies on a summer evening—small flickers surrounded by darkness. I hear "cell-phone" and "home" and then his eyes close again, searching for comfort in a matrix of tangled tubes and thoughts. The time change in hospital country is that time goes faster, meals are sometimes forgotten—worry washing away hunger.

By evening, Audrey and I know we should leave to find dinner outside this white walled country. I worry about how my running shoes will fit in among pointed NYC high heels and Prada bags. Although I carry my small backpack, on this trip childhood baggage has been lost, past hurts are healed. Happy memories with my father soften the blow—Sniffy, the elephant stories, bagels and butter, cigar smoke, and televised football games. Sometimes childhood wounds can be like mud on my running shoes, keeping me stuck when I could fly. Today I have no mud, the trail is clear—love the only markers.

It is late as we're seated at a small table in the corner of my father's favorite restaurant. Audrey tells me, "Always he orders the Veal Parmigiana and Caesar Salad with no croutons." Her menu hides her tears. We have tried to reassure each other all day, passing the comfort baton back and forth. But sometimes the baton is dropped as we face the facts: we all will stop running some day.

I awake the next morning, my last day before

flying home. I decide to run up town to kiss my father goodbye, the soles of my shoes carrying me closer to the soul of a man I will dearly miss someday. I kiss his soft cheek and then run to catch the elevator. When the door closes, I feel grateful to the man who gave me the chance to log so many miles in this beautiful race we call life.

Published in the
Boulder Camera, June 2008

The Housing Crisis

Both my husband and I have parents at the age where they're considering new homes. So in the same week I flew to Florida to visit my father in his new "digs," my husband flew to Texas because his father might need assisted living, and my mother called from D.C. with, "Dear, I really think it might be time for me to move to Boulder."

"Mom, could we talk about that next week?" I feel like a little girl running to keep up on an uneven sidewalk.

I haven't seen my father since we thought we'd lost him in a New York City ICU. He lay amidst tangled tubes and a tangled mind, searching for speech. But he kept fighting, finding his way home with no memory of how lost he was. He sits with me by the pool, his cane leaning against his thin legs. He assures me the clouds are passing and promises I'll go home with a suntan. I decide not to discuss that nowadays too much sun isn't good for us as I recall the needlepoint pillow in his previous home, "You can never be too rich, too thin or too tan."

"You know, I've had three wives, and sometimes I can't remember who I lived with in what house."

Each house marks the change in his life stage, each doorway opening into a world further away from mine. His latest world is decorated by pillboxes on the counter, plastic seats in the shower, and a television so loud we all end up shouting.

"Turn that down!" his wife yells from the kitchen sink."

"What, dear? I can't hear you!"

The phone rings and my father answers, "Hello, hello, who's there?"

Everything we say has to be repeated. Confusion is the new wallpaper. Yet he is still in the stage of knowing what he doesn't know, as he asks, "Which wife did I travel to Africa with?"

I find respite in the guest bedroom, sleeping in a single bed, pillow talk with my husband on my cell phone. His father is also moving, but sadly is facing his final doorway. The TV is no longer loud or even on. At my in-law's home, no one is interested in the outside world. His father's mind is healthy; his body is not. My husband described helping him out of the shower and turning away as he wrapped his father's frail body in dignity with a clean towel. The phone is quiet as I catch a hiccup of tears in his voice. It is like trying to board a moving train with our fathers. They stretch out aging hands we briefly hold, all the while knowing we'll be staying at the station.

My husband and I miss the comfort of our home where the only reminders of growing old are sore muscles and stronger reading glasses. We whisper sweet wishes of growing old differently. We trick ourselves into believing we'll find a way to shield our children from the pain we're feeling.

"Darling, darling!" my father yells from the other room. "Don't go to sleep without kissing us goodnight!" My father's cheek has softened with age and the blue of his eyes are the blue of my children's as infants.

"Sleep tight and thanks for having me," I whisper as I kiss his cheek. My tear christens my Jewish father as I close the door behind me, silently thanking him for the sad yet tender glimpse of the last house on the block.

Published in the
Chicago Tribune, March 2009

Radiating Friendship

I knit on summer evenings. The soft pink wool is slowly becoming a shawl. Although it has the feel of my children's baby blankets, this shawl contains a harsher reality. Each stitch reminds me it's a gift for my friend who's enduring the debilitating effects of chemotherapy and radiation. I'm told one of the side effects is a coldness that enters the body—a cold unforgiving illness. I call them her "healing sessions," trying to soften the language as if to create a gentler journey.

For 16 years we've met once a week for coffee—sharing stories of children, husbands, parents, births, deaths, divorce, bad days, good days, recipes, and real estate. These were our lives, one hour each week, until her sore throat. "The doctor said antibiotics should help." But they didn't help, and then we were no longer talking about someone else's cancer, but her own.

A set of symptoms develop for friends of those with cancer. I'm scared, I don't sleep well, I'm sad, I feel helpless, I'm angry, I worry about my own lymph nodes and freckles on my husbands back—but most of all, I want to help so much that it aches inside. Before she was nauseous every day I baked pumpkin muffins and bought her Starbucks. I gave her sweet smelling cream and soft, purple socks. I call and write emails, send poems and pray. But so often I feel cancer ties our hands, taunting us as we're cornered and powerless.

Her latest email read, "Just wondering if by chance I could take you to breakfast and catch a ride to one of my many doctor's appointments?"

Given she'd been so sick from her treatments, I hadn't seen her as frequently and imagined the worst. But she looked beautiful. The beauty went beyond her pretty face and wisps of curly hair. I saw clarity in her eyes. Here was someone who knew what she wanted: She wanted to live. Blistery burns on her neck left by radiation were the only signs of her painful truth. She gracefully unwrapped her scarf to let me in closer and admitted it had been excruciating, but was slowly healing. For now, because her throat was so sore, she spoke in a quiet, laryngitis voice. I ordered our bagels in the noisy shop, relieved to show my care and concern in such a concrete way—handing her a small plastic knife and napkins like I would for my children. We sat with our bagels and hot tea. She no longer drinks coffee, but sipped her tea along with an 1/8 tsp. of morphine so she could swallow small bites of bagel and cream cheese.

She patiently told me everything, revealing her journey like someone returning from a frightful trip. I listened with a mixture of sadness, fascination, and deep respect for her survival on the cancer trek. Halfway along the trail, she still has major surgery left to remove the tumor from her esophagus. Sometimes she'd write in pretty script on the pad next to her when talking became too tiring. "I'm never scared of dying, just scared of feeling sick forever."

As she talked quietly and ate slowly, I did the same. It felt so peaceful. We talked about how her cancer forced her to take care of herself in the way we did when we were pregnant—naps, gentleness, trying to eat well, depending on others. Birth and death are such powerful teachers.

Her doctor's appointment was quick and her surgery was scheduled for three weeks away. We celebrated having a definite date for an 8-hour surgery to rebuild her esophagus. We've celebrated many things in our friendship, but never esophageal surgery. I drove slowly home, not wanting our outing to end.

As I picked up my knitting that evening, I realized my shawl wasn't so different from a baby blanket. There is a tender feel to birth and death—and both are powerful reminders of the beauty of life and friendship in between.

Published in
Boulder Women's Magazine, October, 2009

Health-y Care

I now know that Rochester, Minnesota is in the *Guinness Book of World Records* for having the largest plastic ear of corn. *National Geographic* ranked it number eight in their recent story about water towers with creative architecture and they now have two Wal-Marts. But it is also the home of the Mayo Clinic where I recently joined my 84-yr-old mother for a hip consultation checking in on the 14th floor, orthopedic wing, south desk. I've always been uncomfortable in hospitals unless I was giving birth. But avoiding illness is no longer possible, as we all face getting older. My mother's news was not surprising as we left weighed down with literature on hip replacement surgery.

"Well that doesn't sound like a good option, maybe they don't know what they're talking about," commented my mother as the elevator door closed shut. "I saw plenty of healthy cartilage on my x-rays!"

"It really was pretty black and white Mom, and I think he's probably seen a lot of hips." I watch my step, not wanting to get in the way of my mother's own footsteps as she maneuvers through old age.

Our trip to Rochester was short and we spent most of our time limping around a beautiful Barnes and Noble taking time to rest in Starbucks. It was actually quite comforting spending time with books and my slow moving mother. The peaceful pace makes me breathe easier. At the same time, the four-block radius of the Mayo clinic is full of young and old in wheel chairs, those with small oxygen tanks, and restaurants that cater to those with special dietary needs—which was not very peaceful. I faced how much I take good health for granted. And how for years I took for granted my parents' capacity for independence.

My mother and I traded off mothering one another.

"Deary, finish more of your chicken and please wear my extra rain jacket."

As we leave the dinner table, I say, "Mom, let me carry your purse and do you need help getting up?"

Fielding phone calls from my siblings concerned about my mother's physical health and my father's cognitive health with no concerning calls from my kids is a new stage. At times overwhelming, at times very sad—I no longer parent adolescents but instead parent parents. It is a grown-up's "tween" years. I heard a comedian recently comment, "I was handed a whole book to understand my flat screen TV, and only a pamphlet when my son was born." And perhaps we have the equivalent of a mere handout when it comes to our elderly parents.

The health care crisis is a constant concern for all of us but for these two days, the debate wasn't political. It was an internal struggle as I watched my athletic mother have difficulty bending to tie her shoe and climbing in to the airport shuttle. No matter what new programs are developed, hips and minds get old. It becomes an individual struggle in all of us as we question how to "care" for the "health" of our elderly parents. How to help without intruding? How to support without trying to rescue? How to listen without believing my answers are the right ones? My hope is I've learned some of the answers from my own kids.

As always I find myself rushing to catch the plane when I leave either parent—wanting to leave but am never quite ready, believing I can fix something in the last few minutes. But I have to remind myself that parenting isn't so much about fixing but more about just showing up—no matter who we are parenting surrounded by the books and stories of our individual lives.

Published in
the *Boulder Camera,* October 2009

A Mother's Knitting

My 83-year-old mother is coming to town this week, and she won't be leaving. She has always loved Boulder, visiting us at least two times a year, making the trek from the east coast for long weekends. That way we could enjoy each other without making each other crazy.

"Deary, you never make me crazy, but I know I make you crazy," she always reminds me.

They say it's best for the elderly to make their final move while they have their wits about them. My mother has more than her wits about her—as she prefers to run errands by bicycle, take as many courses as possible, hike the English countryside and most recently design a web site with a political focus. She's thrilled about the Bolder Boulder, the Shakespeare Festival, and CU Continuing Education. Suddenly I wonder if I'll be able to keep up with her. My husband and I cherish quiet solitude, reading the NY Times, long runs, and the excitement of a good thriller at the movie theater. Our Friday and Saturday nights are devoted to fielding phone calls from our fifteen-year-old daughter whose plans are constantly changing—all related to parties, sleepovers, and other requests testing how anxious she can make us by evening's end.

Adding my mother to the mix is like making up a new cookie recipe. The ingredients sound okay but I'm not quite sure how it'll turn out. And really the old recipe was working just fine. For 30 years I've kept a comfortable distance from my mother. Having ten states between us is my daughter's version of closing her bedroom door and text messaging. I'm quickly trying to learn this new dance of motherhood. As my daughter twirls away, I twirl closer to my own mother, one step, two-step, clap and back again. It is a dance to both classical music in the living room and the beat of my daughter's rap music upstairs.

My mother once asked, "Is that someone yelling?"

I answered, "No mom, that's music."

I drive by her new home, stopping long enough to imagine her tending the garden in a floppy hat and too short khakis, reading on the front porch only a few miles away from me—forever. Just as I walked in to my children's room before they were born, wondering what it would be like to have a new life fill the space. How do I get ready for my mother to join my world as I joined her over fifty years ago?

As with our children, we learn as we go, being both teacher and student. I thought about the soft blue scarf I'm knitting, uncertain of how to "cast off." My mother knows; she'll teach me like I read on-line. Casting off is an important stitch of binding the wool so it doesn't fray when your project is complete. Perhaps mothers and daughters are always learning to "cast off" from one another, completing one stage and moving to the next, trusting things will not unravel, but instead holding onto the beauty of a new beginning.

Published in the
Christian Science Monitor, May 2009

Driving Across the Divide

When my daughter was small she once asked, "When did you become all grown-up?"

Years later I can finally answer. As she proudly slides her new driver's license into the small plastic sleeve of her pink wallet, becoming the newest driver in our family, and my elderly father sadly removes his license from his worn leather billfold, I realize I am now a grown-up. I wave goodbye to both children and parents as I search for a brake that is absent. I'm standing in the middle of a country road where my children brush by—heading for tomorrow and my parents pass in the other direction, fall foliage outlining the colors of change.

My daughter is my youngest and the last of my three children to drive. Both the relief and accomplishment of nearing the end of those "gripping the dashboard" training sessions felt like my crossing over point.

Our first lessons were around the neighborhood where my kids, each in their own time, inched forward, peering over the steering wheel as I breathed deeply—like moments during labor where the breath helps to welcome the separation from our children. Main roads brought deeper breathing, tighter gripping, imagined breaking, and wilder hand gestures that inevitably led to, "Mom, stop doing that, you're making things worse!"

My husband has been relegated to the back seat, because my behavior pales in comparison to his overall panic when my daughter is behind the wheel. And my father's stop and go driving and swerving moments were no easier for us to manage. Adulthood is giving our children the gift of independence while simultaneously helping our parents face their increased dependence. It is a grown-up's "tween" years.

My father sent my husband and sons sweaters from his closet. I smell his aftershave in the worn wool. "I don't need winter clothing anymore," he confides and I decide not to ask why. My daughter buys new sweaters for school and I buy Tampax to put under her sink, no longer needing them in our bathroom closet. All are road markers pointing to the freedom, glory and inevitable losses of my life as a grown-up.

The phone rings more often these days, both my parents checking in for comfort. "Deary, I just like to hear your voice," confides my 84-year-old mother. My father calls to repeat the conversation we had the day before. I say, "Yes, Dad, we received the sweaters and thanks a lot," knowing I'll repeat the same thank you tomorrow. Perhaps many "thank-yous" are what he needs—just to know he's given enough before he can rest. My daughter calls, asking permission to keep the car later into the evening and promises to be home by midnight. "Thank you," she says, and I too cherish feeling appreciated as I sit in the swivel chair of adulthood at our family switchboard.

My daughter is absorbed in My Space as I practice my handstand for yoga class against her bedroom wall. My t-shirt rides up, revealing my small breasts in comparison to my daughter's full bosoms. Nourishing my daughter has now become a letting go, while still holding on. It's a grown up handstand—an upside down balancing act where my perspective shifts as I search for balance; pulled by parents and children, forever trying to hold myself straight and strong.

When the kids were young, life moved so quickly, time for self contemplation and reflection only lasted as long as a child's nap, an unaccompanied birthday party, morning kindergarten, a swim lesson, or a morning cup of coffee before I'd hear, "Momma, momma!" and I was once again embracing a little one and my role as a young mother. I may have appeared grown-up to others, but to myself I was always reaching for that moment where I felt confident in balancing life's ceramic plates decorated with images of a woman, a mother, a wife, a psychologist, a writer, an athlete and so much more. When I could manage it all with grace—then I'd be a grown-up.

But it was only as my daughter pulled the car in to a parking space, making sure to stay in the lines that I felt I'd arrived. As she evened her way in, the lines on either side let her know she was there. For me, the line drawn by my children as they grow up and the line set by my parents as they grow old guides me toward that in-between space of my life as a grown-up—a space marked by both freedom and responsibility and the beauty of gracefully growing along with those around me.

About the Author

Dr. Dann-Courtney has had a full-time psychotherapy private practice for close to 20 years, specializing in eating disorders, treating adolescents and adults. She teaches graduate students and other professionals. Over 40 of her essays about family life have been published in national newspapers and magazines. She lives with her husband and three children in Boulder, Colorado.

Available from NorlightsPress and fine booksellers everywhere

Toll free: 888-558-4354   **Online:** www.norlightspress.com

Shipping Info: Add $2.95 for first item and $1.00 for each additional item

Name _____

Address _____

Daytime Phone _____

E-mail _____

No. Copies	Title	Price (each)	Total Cost
		Subtotal	
		Shipping	
		Total	

Payment by (circle one):

   Check   Visa   Mastercard   Discover   Am Express

Card number_____3 digit code_____

Exp.date_____ Signature_____

Mailing Address:

762 State Road 458
Bedford, IN 47421

Sign up to receive our catalogue at www.norlightspress.com

Made in the USA
Lexington, KY
06 March 2012